Guiding Those Left Behind In Oklahoma

LEGAL AND PRACTICAL THINGS
YOU NEED TO DO
TO SETTLE AN ESTATE IN OKLAHOMA

and

HOW TO ARRANGE YOUR OWN AFFAIRS
TO AVOID UNNECESSARY COSTS
TO YOUR FAMILY

AF694543

By AMELIA E. POHL, ESQ.

and Oklahoma Attorney
LARRY PARMAN

EAGLE PUBLISHING COMPANY OF BOCA

Copyright © 2005 by AMELIA E. POHL
All rights reserved.

No part of this book may be reproduced or transmitted for any purpose, in any form and by any means, graphic, electronic or mechanical, including photocopying, recording, or by any information storage or retrieval system, without permission in writing from AMELIA E. POHL.

The purpose of this book is to provide the reader with an informative overview of the subject; but laws change frequently and are subject to different interpretations as courts rule on the meaning or effect of a law. This book is sold with the understanding that neither the authors, nor the editors, nor the publisher, nor the distributors of this book are engaging in, or rendering, legal, accounting, financial planning, medical, or any other professional service. If you need legal, accounting, medical, financial planning or any other expert advice, you should seek the services of a licensed professional.

This book is intended for use by the consumer for his or her own benefit. If you use this book to counsel someone about the law or tax matters, then that may be considered to be an unauthorized and illegal practice.

WEB SITES: Web sites appear throughout the book. These Web sites are offered for the convenience of the reader only. Publication of these Web site addresses is not an endorsement by the authors, editors or publishers of this book.

EAGLE PUBLISHING COMPANY OF BOCA
4199 N. Dixie Highway, #2
Boca Raton, FL 33431 E-mail: info@eaglepublishing.com

Printed in the United States of America
ISBN 1-892407-84-1
Library of Congress Catalog Card Number 2002095161

Guiding Those Left Behind In Oklahoma

CONTENTS

About The Book

We tried to make this book as comprehensive as possible so there are specialized sections of the book that do not apply to the general population and may not be of interest to you. The following GUIDE POSTS appear throughout the book. You can read the section if the situation applies to you or skip the section if it doesn't. Skipping the section will not affect the continuity of the book.

GUIDE POSTS

SPOUSE

The SPOUSE POST means that the information provided is specifically for the spouse of the decedent. If the decedent was single, you can skip this section.

☎ LAWYER

The CALL-A-LAWYER POST alerts you to a situation that may require the assistance of an attorney. See the end of this chapter for information about how to find a lawyer.

CAUTION

The CAUTION POST alerts you to a potential problem. It is followed by a suggestion about how to avoid the problem.

Special Situation

The SPECIAL SITUATION POST means that the information given in that paragraph applies to a particular event or situation; for example when the decedent dies a violent death. If the situation does not apply, you can skip the section.

The Organization of the Book

Guiding Those Left Behind refers to the things that need to be done in order to settle an Estate in Oklahoma. The purpose of this book is to guide the reader through that process. It explains:

1. How to tend to the funeral and burial
2. What agencies need to be notified
3. How to locate the decedent's property
4. What bills need (and do not need) to be paid
5. How to determine who is entitled to inherit the decedent's property
6. How to transfer the decedent's property to the proper beneficiary

We devoted a chapter to each of these 6 steps; and for those who are in charge of settling an Estate, we placed a CHECK LIST at the end of Chapter 6 summarizing those things that need to be done. Once you read Chapters 1 through 6 you will be able to identify those problems that can happen when someone dies. Using those Chapters as a base, you can set up your own Estate Plan so that your family is not burdened by similar problems. The rest of the book (Chapters 7, 8 and 9) suggests different methods you can use to accomplish this goal.

GLOSSARY

This book is designed for the average reader. Legal terminology has been kept to a minimum. There is a glossary at the end of the book in the event you come across a legal term that is not familiar to you.

FICTITIOUS NAMES AND EVENTS

The examples in this book are based loosely on actual events; however, all names are fictitious; and the events, as portrayed, are fictitious.

Reading the Law

Where applicable, we identified the state statute or federal statute that is the basis of the discussion. We did this as a reference, and also to encourage the general public to read the law as it is written. Prior to the Internet the only way you could look up the law was to physically take yourself to the local courthouse law library or the law section of a public library. Today all of the state and federal statutes are literally at your finger tips. They are just a mouse click away on the Internet.

To look up the law all you need is the address of the Web site and the identifying number of the statute.

FEDERAL STATUTES
http://www4.law.cornell.edu/uscode

OKLAHOMA STATUTES
http://oklegal.onenet.net

The Oklahoma legislature has arranged their statutes into 85 Titles, e.g. Title 47 is Motor Vehicles. Title 58 is Probate Procedure, and so on.

Each Title is divided into numbered Sections. Some Sections are further divided into Parts. We will identify the statute by the number of the Title and the Section and Part. For example, (OS 63-1-317(c)) refers to Oklahoma Statute, Title 63, Section 1, Part 317, paragraph (c). To look up the statute, go to the Oklahoma Statute Web site and type 63-1-317 in the search box.

You may find it both interesting and profitable to read the law as it is actually written, if you come across a topic in the book that is important to you.

Larry Parman, Esq.

His law firm is now one of the Midwest's leading estate planning law firms with offices in Oklahoma City, Kansas City, Tulsa and Hayes. The firms's primary focus is on estate planning and asset protection. You can learn more about the law firm from their Web site:

www.parmanlaw.com

LARRY PARMAN received his Juris Doctorate from the University of Missouri-Kansas City in 1974. He is an Accredited Estate Planner with the National Association of Estate Planners and Councils.

Mr. Parman is a registered securities representative with the National Association of Securities Dealers and has an extensive background, which he puts to use in preparing practical, understandable, estate plans for his clients.

Mr. Parman is the founder of the law firm of PARMAN & Associates.

In addition to his practice and regular schedule of educational seminars, Mr. Parman is a frequent guest on radio and can be seen on television talk shows explaining the importance of proper estate planning. Prosperity Productions selected Mr. Parman as a featured speaker in their nationally recognized educational video on Living Trusts. Mr. Parman has been a member of the board of Oklahoma's City Junior Achievement chapter for the past decade, serving two terms as president.

LARRY PARMAN is also a member of the AMERICAN ACADEMY OF ESTATE PLANNING ATTORNEYS.

About the Academy

The American Academy of Estate Planning Attorneys is a member organization serving the needs of legal professionals concentrating on Estate Planning. Through the Academy's comprehensive training and educational programs on state-of-the-art Estate Planning law and techniques, it fosters excellence in Estate Planning among its members and helps them deliver the highest possible service to their clients. The Academy provides its members with excellent legal education, and top notch practice management support. In addition, each member is required to attain thirty-six units of continuing legal education in tax and Estate Planning annually.

The American Academy of Estate Planning Attorneys serves law firms in over 150 geographic areas in forty-four states. Clients who chose an attorney who is a member of the Academy can feel confident that they have an attorney who is dedicated to bringing them the highest quality of service.

The Academy is also committed to educating consumers on vital Estate Planning issues that touch their lives. Through its series of publications, educational programs and its consumer Web site, the Academy seeks to create a public armed with the information they need to become wise consumers of Estate Planning services.

THE AMERICAN ACADEMY OF
ESTATE PLANNING ATTORNEYS
http://www.aaepa.com

Amelia E. Pohl, Esq.

Before becoming an attorney in 1985, AMELIA E. POHL taught mathematics on both the high school and college level. During her tenure as Associate Professor of Mathematics at Prince George's Community College in Maryland, she wrote several books including

Probability: A Set Theory Approach
Principals of Counting
Common Stock Sense.

During her practice of law Attorney Pohl observed that many people want to reduce the high cost of legal fees by performing or assisting with their own legal transactions. Attorney Pohl found that, with a bit of guidance, people are able to perform many legal transactions for themselves. Attorney Pohl utilizes her background as teacher, author and attorney to provide that "bit of guidance" to the general public in the form of self-help legal books that she has written. Amelia E. Pohl is currently "translating" this book for the remaining 49 states:

Guiding Those Left Behind in Maine
Guiding Those Left Behind In North Dakota
Guiding Those Left Behind In Wyoming, etc.

THE DESIGN ARTIST

LUBOSH CECH designed the cover of this book. He is a renowned artist, with extensive educational background and professional work experience. He studied design, applied art, and painting in his native Prague, Czech Republic. He also studied art in Italy at University of Bologna. Since moving to the United States in 1984, Mr. Cech has been designing art exhibitions, working as an art director, and graphic designer. Mr. Cech is a photographer and often incorporates his photographs into his art work.

Lubosh Cech is the founder of OKO DESIGN STUDIO located in Portland, Oregon. He designs promotional materials for print and digital media. He has received numerous rewards for both graphic design and painting. For more information about Mr. Cech and the OKO Design Studio visit his Web site.

http://www.okodesignstudio.com

The photograph on the cover was provided by the Nebraska Game and Parks Commission.

ACKNOWLEDGMENT

When someone dies, the family attorney is often among the first to be called. Family members have questions about whether probate is necessary, who to notify, how to get possession of the assets, etc. Over the years, as we practiced in the field of Elder Law, we noticed that the questions raised were much the same family to family. We both agreed that a book answering such questions would be of service to the general public.

We also observed, that those who had experience in settling the estate of a loved one were more understanding of the process, and better able to make decisions about how to arrange their own finances to avoid problems that could arise in settling an estate. We named the book ***Guiding Those Left Behind***. The "Guiding" refers to the guidance that this book gives in the event that you need to settle the Estate of your loved one. It also refers to the guidance that you can give to your family by setting up your own Estate Plan so that your family is not burdened by unnecessary costs and delays in settling your estate.

We wish to thank all of the clients, whom we have had the honor and pleasure to serve, for providing us with the impetus to produce this book.

When You Need A Lawyer

The purpose of the book is to give the reader a basic understanding of what needs to be done when someone dies, and to provide information about how a person can arrange his own affairs to avoid problems for his own family. It is not intended as a substitute for legal counsel or any other kind of professional advice. If you have any legal question, then you should to seek the counsel of an attorney. When looking for an attorney, consider three things: EXPERTISE, COST and PERSONALITY.

EXPERTISE

The Oklahoma Bar does not have a program to certify that an attorney is specialized in a particular area of law. This being the case, an attorney in Oklahoma may not represent to the public that he/she is certified by the state as a specialist in any given area of law. Attorneys are allowed to state that they concentrate on certain areas of law or that they limit their practice to an area of law.

The Oklahoma Bar Association has a Lawyer Referral Service. You can call them at (918) 584-5243 and they will refer you to an attorney in your area who practices the type of law that you seek. There is a $20 fee for the referral and initial half hour consultation.

One of the most reliable ways to find an attorney is through personal referral. Ask your friends, family or business acquaintances if they used an attorney for the field of law that you seek and whether they were pleased with the results. It is important to employ an attorney who is experienced in the area of law you seek. Your friend may have a wonderful Estate Planning attorney, but if you suffered an injury to your body, you need an attorney who is experienced in Personal Injury.

Before employing an attorney for a job, ask how long he has practiced that type of law and what percentage of his practice is devoted to that type of law.

COST

In addition to the attorney's experience, it is important to check what it will cost in attorney's fees. When you call for an appointment ask what the attorney will charge for the initial consultation and the approximate cost for the service you seek. Ask whether there will be additional costs such as filing fees, accounting fees, expert witness fees, etc.

If the least expensive attorney is out of your price range, you can call your local county Bar Association for the telephone number of the Legal Services office nearest you.

The Oklahoma Bar Association has a directory of Legal Services Programs located throughout the state at its Web site.

OKLAHOMA BAR ASSOCIATION
http://www.okbar.org

PERSONALITY

Of equal importance to the attorney's experience and legal fees, is your relationship with the attorney. How easy was it to reach the attorney? Did you go through layers of receptionists and legal assistants before being allowed to speak to the attorney? Did the attorney promptly return your call? If you had difficulty reaching the attorney, then you can expect similar problems should you employ that attorney.

Did the attorney treat you with respect? Did the attorney treat you paternally with a "father knows best" attitude or did he treat you as an intelligent person with the ability to understand the options available to you and the ability to make your own decision based on the information provided to you?

Are you able to understand and easily communicate with the attorney? Is he speaking to you in plain English or is his explanation of the matter so full of legalese to be almost meaningless to you?

Do you find the attorney's personality to be pleasant or grating? Sometimes people rub each other the wrong way. It is like rubbing a cat the wrong way. Stroking a cat from head to tail is pleasing to the cat, but petting it in the opposite direction, no matter how well intended, causes friction. If the lawyer makes you feel annoyed or uncomfortable, then find another attorney.

It is worth the effort to take the time to interview as many attorneys as it takes to find one with the right expertise, fee schedule and personality for you.

The First Week 1

Dealing with the death of a close family member or friend is difficult. Not only do you need to deal with your own emotions, but often with those of your family and friends. Sometimes their sorrow is more painful to you, than what you are experiencing yourself.

In addition to the emotional impact of a death, there are many things that need to be done, from arranging the funeral and burial, to closing out the business affairs of the ***decedent*** (the person who died) and finally giving whatever property is left to the proper beneficiary.

The funeral and burial take only a few days. Wrapping up the affairs of the decedent may take considerably longer. This chapter explains what things you (the spouse or closest family member) need to do during the first week, beginning at the moment of death and continuing through the funeral.

> ♀ MALE GENDER USED ♂
>
> Rather than use "he/she" or "his/her" for simplicity (and hoping not to offend anyone) we will refer to the decedent and his Personal Representative using the male gender.
>
> References to other people will be in both genders.

AUTOPSIES

In today's high tech world of medicine, doctors are fairly certain of the cause of death, but if there is a question as to the cause of death, the doctor may ask anyone who is taking responsibility for the burial: parent, surviving spouse, child, guardian, next of kin, to give written consent for an autopsy. If none of these are available, then a friend, or whoever has legal responsibility for the burial may give permission (OS 21-1154(B)(3)).

The person who authorizes the autopsy must agree to pay for it because the cost of the examination is not covered under most health insurance plans. And that cost could be sizeable, running anywhere from several hundred to several thousand dollars, but it may be in the family's best interest to consent to the autopsy. The examination might reveal a genetic disorder that could be treated if it later appears in another family member. Death from a car "accident" could have been a heart attack at the wheel. Perhaps the patient who died suddenly in a hospital was misdiagnosed. The nursing home resident could have died from neglect and not old age. Even if none of these are found, knowing the cause of death with certainty is better than not knowing.

That was the case with the family of a woman who was taken to the hospital complaining of stomach pains. The doctors thought she might be suffering from gallbladder disease but she died before they could effectively treat her. A doctor suggested that an autopsy be performed to determine the actual cause of death. The woman had three daughters, one of whom objected to the autopsy: "Why spend that kind of money? It won't bring Mom back."

The daughter's wishes were respected, however over the years as they aged and became ill with their own various ailments, they would undergo physical examinations. As part of taking their medical history, doctors routinely asked "And what was the cause of your mother's death?"

None could answer the question.

This is not a dramatic story. No mysterious genetic disorder ever occurred in any of her daughters, nor in any of their children. But each daughter (including the one who objected) at some point in her life, was confronted with the nagging question "What did Mom die of?"

AUTOPSIES PERFORMED BY MEDICAL EXAMINER

When a person dies, a physician must, within 48 hours of the death (or discovery of the body) sign a medical certification stating the cause of death (OS 63-1-317(c)). This is not a problem if a person dies in a hospital or nursing home from natural causes. If he dies at home and the death was expected, the treating physician can be contacted to sign the medical certificate verifying that the decedent died of natural causes. But if a person dies, suddenly, at home, and he was not under the care of a physician, whoever discovers the body must call 911 to summon the police. The law enforcement officer will call the Medical Examiner to determine the cause of death.

If the death occurred under questionable circumstances the family can request that the County conduct the autopsy. If the Medical Examiner agrees, there will be no charge to the decedent's family or to his Estate. However, if that is not an option, and the family wants an autopsy, whoever authorizes the procedure is responsible for payment.

The Medical Examiner will investigate the following:

- ⇨ deaths that are suspicious or unusual
- ⇨ violent deaths whether by homicide, suicide, or accident
- ⇨ deaths that might pose a threat to public health
- ⇨ when the decedent was not under the care of a physician and there was no medical history to indicate the cause of death
- ⇨ death of any inmate while in police custody
- ⇨ death of anyone whose body is to be cremated, buried at sea, or transported out of state.

The Medical Examiner will order an autopsy whenever he thinks it in the public interest to do so. The next of kin can have their own physician present at the autopsy, if they wish. Once the examination is finished, the Medical Examiner will send the report to the District Attorney who is investigating the case (OS 63-945).

Should an autopsy be necessary, the Medical Examiner will take possession of the body. It will not be released until the examination is complete. Meanwhile, the family can proceed with funeral arrangements. The funeral director will contact the Medical Examiner to determine when he can pick up the body and proceed with the funeral.

AUTOPSIES PERFORMED BY THE INSURANCE COMPANY

A company that issues an accident or health insurance policy in Oklahoma has the right to include a provision in the policy giving the company authority to perform an autopsy on the deceased insured person (OS 36-4405A(10)). The cost of the autopsy must be paid for by the insurance company, so they will not order an autopsy unless there is some important reason to do so, such as whether the cause of death is covered under that policy.

ANATOMICAL GIFTS

Hospital personnel determine whether a mortally ill patient is a candidate for an organ donation. Early on in the donor program those over 65 were not considered as suitable candidates. Today, however, the condition of the organ, and not the age, is the determining factor.

The federal government has established regional Organ Procurement Organizations throughout the United States to coordinate the donor program. THE LIFE SHARE TRANSPLANT DONOR SERVICE OF OKLAHOMA located in Oklahoma City is the Organ Procurement Organization for the state. If it is decided that the patient is a candidate, the hospital will contact the Donor Service. The Life Share Transplant Donor Service, together with the doctor who is treating the patient, will determine whether the patient is a suitable donor.

GIFT AUTHORIZED PRIOR TO DEATH

The decedent may have signed an Organ Donor Card and made that notation on his driver's license. Such anatomical gifts are recorded in the Oklahoma LIFE SHARE DONOR REGISTRY. This information is available to the Oklahoma Organ Sharing Network. Instead of indicating his donation on his driver's license, he may have included an anatomical gift as part of his ADVANCE DIRECTIVE FOR HEALTH CARE. In such case, the gift is probably not part of the Life Share Donor Registry and the hospital personnel or the donor's doctor need to be made aware of the gift in quick proximity to the time of death — preferably before death. If it is determined that the donation is medically acceptable, the gift will be made. No family member need give permission, provided the hospital has a copy of the decedent's unrevoked donor card (OS 63-2211, 63-2220.10, 63-3101.4).

GIFT AUTHORIZED BY THE FAMILY

If no donor card is on record, and it is determined that the decedent is a suitable donor, the hospital administrator, or his representative will approach the family to request permission for the donation (OS 63-2214). Oklahoma statute states an order of priority for those who can give permission:

1st spouse
2nd adult son or daughter
3rd either parent
4th adult brother or sister
5th the guardian of the decedent at time of death
6th anyone who is authorized to dispose of the body

Every effort must be made to contact those people with highest priority. No gift can be made if someone agrees to the gift and someone with higher priority objects. For example, if the sister of the decedent agrees to the gift (4th in priority) and the decedent had an adult child (2nd in priority), the child needs to be made aware of the gift. If the child objects, then no gift can be made. Similarly, the statute prohibits the gift if the decedent, prior to death, refused to make a gift, or ever expressed an objection to someone with authority to make the gift (OS 63-2203(B)).

AFTER THE DONATION

Once the donation is made the body is delivered to the funeral home and prepared for burial or cremation as directed by the family. The donation does not disfigure the body so there can be an open casket viewing if the family so wishes. Some regional Organ Procurement Organizations have an aftercare program that includes a letter of condolence to the family and an expression of gratitude for the gift. For privacy reasons, the identity of the recipient of the gift is not disclosed, but on request from the family, the local Organ Procurement Organization will give the family basic demographic information about the donation, such as the age, sex, marital status, number of children and occupation of the recipient of the gift.

GIFT FOR EDUCATION OR RESEARCH

Consider offering to release the body for the purpose of education or research in the event that the decedent signed a donor card, but was not an appropriate candidate for an organ donation. You can offer to release the body to a school of medicine.

The University of Oklahoma (405) 271-2424
Health Science Center, Willed Body Program
P.O. Box 26901
Oklahoma City, OK 73190

Oklahoma College of Osteopathic Medicine (918) 582-1972
Anatomy Department
1111 West 17th Street
Tulsa, OK 74107

The Oklahoma College of Osteopathic Medicine requires that the decedent registered for the program prior to death. They will not accept a donation from the next of kin. Procedures at the University of Oklahoma are different. They prefer advance registration, but will consider donations from whoever is in charge of disposing of the body. The school will pay for the transportation of the body provided it is within the state of Oklahoma.

You will need to call the school as soon as possible after the death to see if the school will accept the body. In general, they will refuse a body if the decedent was obese or if he died from a contagious disease or from a crushing injury.

The study can take up to two years to complete. At the end of the study the remains are cremated. The ***cremains*** (cremated remains) will be placed in a cemetery that is local to the university; or if the family wishes, the cremains will be delivered to the next of kin.

CAVEAT: Federal law prohibits payment for organ donations (42 U.S.C. 274 e). There is no ban on payments made to prepare organs or tissue for transplantation, nor is there any ban on charges made to transport bodies or body parts. Not-for-profit, as well as for-profit, companies have sprung up that are in the business of preparing and delivering body parts. These companies request donations from families — so they are not violating federal law by paying for the donation. The company prepares the body tissue or other parts of the donated body, and then distributes the parts throughout the United States to physicians, hospitals, research centers, etc. In many cases the monies charged for preparation and transportation includes a sizable profit.

If a company or organization other than Life Share Transplant Donor Service approaches you to make a donation, before agreeing, you may want to learn about the company that is requesting the donation.

What is the name of the company?
Where are their main headquarters located?
What is their primary business activity?
What is the name and job description of the person making the request?

DETERMINE THE END USE OF THE DONATION

You may want to ask what they intend to do with the tissue or body part. If it is being used for research, then what type of research? Where is the research being conducted? If it will be used for transplantation, then what agency (doctor, hospital) will receive the donation and where is that agency located?

Once you have this information you can make an informed decision as to whether you wish to make the donation to that organization.

THE FUNERAL

Approximately ten percent of deaths occur suddenly because of accident, suicide, foul play or undetected illness. But, in general, death occurs after a lengthy illness, with a common scenario being that of an aged person who dies after being ill for several months, if not years. In such case, family and friends are prepared for the happening. Expected or not, the first job is the disposition of the body.

THE PREARRANGED FUNERAL

Increasingly, people are arranging, in advance, for their own funeral and burial. This makes it easier on the family both financially and emotionally. All the decisions have been made and there is no guessing what the decedent would have wanted.

If the decedent made provision for his burial, you should come across a cemetery deed or perhaps a certificate for a burial plot. If he made provision for his funeral, you should find a PREPAID FUNERAL BENEFITS contract. You need to read the contract to determine what provisions were made. If the contract was paid by installments, you need to determine whether it is paid in full. You also need to find out whether the contract was a fixed price agreement or whether there will be additional charges.

If you cannot locate the contract, but you know the decedent made provision for his burial and funeral, call the funeral home and ask them to send you a copy of the contract. If you believe the decedent purchased a funeral plan but you do not know the name of the funeral home, then call the local funeral homes. Many local funeral homes are owned by national firms with computer capacity to identify people who have purchased a contract at any of their many locations.

Once you have possession of the Agreement, take it with you to the funeral home and go over the terms of the Agreement with the funeral director. Inquire whether there will be any charge that is not included in the contract.

MAKING FUNERAL ARRANGEMENTS

If the decedent died unexpectedly or without having made any prior funeral arrangements then your first job is to choose a funeral director and make arrangements for the funeral or cremation. Most people choose the nearest or most conveniently located funeral home without comparison shopping. However prices for these services can vary significantly from funeral home to funeral home. Savings can be had if you take the time to make a few phone calls.

Receiving price quotes by telephone is your right under Federal law. Federal Trade Commission ("FTC") Rule 453.2 (b) (1) requires a funeral director to give an accurate telephone quote of the prices of his goods and services. Funeral homes are listed in the telephone directory under FUNERAL DIRECTORS. If you live in a small town, there may be only one or two listings. If such is the case, then check out some funeral homes in the next largest city.

Funeral directors usually provide the following services:

- arrange for the transportation of the body to the funeral home and then to the burial site
- obtain burial transit permits
- arrange for the embalming or cremation of the body
- arrange funeral and memorial services and the viewing of the body
- obtain information for the death certificate
- order copies of the death certificate for the family
- have memorial cards printed.

To compare prices you will need to determine:

- ✧ what is included in the price of a basic funeral plan
- ✧ whether you can expect any additional cost.

It may be necessary to have the body embalmed if you are going to have a viewing. Embalming is not necessary if you order a direct cremation or an immediate burial without a viewing. Federal Trade Commission Rule 453.5 prohibits the funeral home from charging an embalming fee unless you order the service.

If the decedent did not own a burial space, then that cost must be included when making funeral arrangements.

PURCHASING THE CASKET

When comparison-shopping, you will find that the single most expensive item in the funeral arrangement is the casket. Most funeral directors will quote you a price for a basic funeral plan that does not include the cost of the casket. Directors usually quote a range of prices for the casket, saying that you will need to come in and choose the casket at the time you contract for the funeral.

When selecting a casket you need to be aware that there may be a considerable mark-up in the price quoted by the funeral director. You do not need to go "sole source" when purchasing the casket. You can purchase the casket elsewhere and have it delivered to the funeral home to be used instead of the one offered by the funeral director. Funeral homes are required to accept caskets purchased elsewhere, and they may not charge a handling fee for accepting that casket. But if the price list given to you by the funeral home states that the price of their casket includes a specific dollar amount for basic services, then the funeral director is allowed to add that dollar amount to the charge for his services, should you purchase the casket elsewhere (FTC Rule 453.2(b), 453.4(2)(A)).

Caskets are not usually displayed for sale in a shopping mall, so most of us have no idea of the going price for a casket. With the advent of the Internet, you can learn all about the cost of any item, even a casket, by using your search engine to find a retail casket sales dealer. If you are not computer literate, you can locate the nearest retail casket sales outlet by looking in the yellow pages under CASKETS. You may need to look in the telephone directory for the nearest large city to find a listing. By making a call to a retail casket sales dealer, you will become knowledgeable in the price range of caskets. You can then decide what is a reasonable price for the product you seek.

The best time to do your comparison shopping is before you go to the funeral home to arrange for the funeral. Once you have determined what you should pay for the casket, it is only fair to give the funeral director the opportunity to meet that price. If you cannot reach a meeting of the minds, then you can always order the casket from the retail sales dealer and have it delivered to the funeral home.

ON-LINE FUNERAL SERVICES

The Internet is changing the way the world does business, and the funeral industry is no exception. A growing number of mortuaries are offering live Webcasts of funerals and wakes for those who are unable to pay their respects in person.

There are Web sites where you can post an obituary. There are on-line memorial chat rooms as well as on-line eulogies and testimonials. There is even a Web site that offers a posthumous e-mail service which allows people to leave final messages for friends and relatives. You can locate these services using your favorite search engine and typing in "obituaries."

THE CREMATION

Increasingly people are opting for cremation. Based on statistics published by the CREMATION ASSOCIATION OF NORTH AMERICA, over 18% of those who died in Oklahoma in the year 2003 were cremated. The reasons for choosing cremation are varied, but for the majority, it is a matter of finances. The cost of cremation is approximately one-sixth that of an ordinary funeral and burial. A major saving is the cost of the casket. No casket is necessary for the cremation and Federal law prohibits a Funeral Director from saying that a casket is required for a direct cremation (FTC Rule 453.3 (b)ii). You may need a suitable container to deliver the body to the crematory. After the cremation, you will need an urn for the ashes.

If you are having a memorial service in a place of worship and no viewing of the body before the cremation, then consider contracting with a facility that does cremations only. Look in the telephone book under CREMATION SERVICES. You will also see cremation "societies" in the telephone book. Some are for-profit and others non-profit. You can also find advertisements for cremation services on the Internet.

PERMIT REQUIRED

Under Oklahoma law a permit from the Medical Examiner must be obtained in order to cremate the decedent. Before proceeding with the cremation, the person in charge of the disposition of the body will need to complete an application-permit form provided by the Office of the Chief Medical Examiner and pay for the permit. The cost of the permit in the year 2005 is $100 (OS 63-1-329.1).

THE OVERWEIGHT DECEDENT

If the decedent weighs more than 300 pounds, then you need to check to see if the Cremation service has facilities large enough to handle the body. If you cannot locate a crematory that can accommodate the body, you will need to make burial arrangements.

THE DECEDENT WITH A PACEMAKER

Cremating a body with a pacemaker or any radiation producing device can cause damage to the cremation chamber or to the person performing the cremation. If the decedent was wearing such electronic aid, then you need to investigate the cost of having it removed prior to the cremation. Some Veterinarian hospitals are implanting used pacemakers into pets who are suffering from heart disease. You might consider asking a Veterinarian to remove the pacemaker in exchange for a donation of the pacemaker to the hospital.

DISPOSING OF THE CREMAINS

If the cremains are to be placed in a cemetery, you need to obtain a suitable urn for the burial. The container provided by the crematory can be used, or you can purchase an urn from the funeral director or crematory service director. Urns cost much less than caskets, but they can cost several hundred dollars. You may wish to do some comparison shopping by calling a retail sales casket dealer.

Many cemeteries have a separate building called a *columbarium,* which is especially designed to store urns. Some cemeteries allow the cremains of a family member to be placed in an occupied family plot or mausoleum. If you wish to have the cremains placed in an occupied mausoleum or family plot, you need to call the cemetery and ask them to explain their policy as it relates to the burial of urns in occupied sites.

Special Situation THE OUT OF STATE BURIAL

If the decedent is to be buried in another state, you will need to arrange for the transportation of the body to that state. Many states, including Oklahoma, require a *Burial Transit Permit* for burial or removal from the state where the death occurred (OS 63-101, 63-1-319). If services are to be held in Oklahoma and in another state, your local funeral director can make arrangements with the out-of-state funeral home for the transportation of the body.

If you do not plan to have funeral services in Oklahoma, you can contact the out-of-state funeral director and ask him to effect the transfer. Many funeral homes belong to a national network of funeral homes, so both the local and the out-of-state funeral director usually have the means to make arrangements to transport the body.

TRANSPORTING CREMAINS

If the body has been cremated, you can transport the cremains yourself, either by carrying the ashes as part of your carry-on luggage or by arranging with the airline to transport the ashes as cargo. Have a certified copy of the death certificate and the Burial Transit Permit ready in the event that you need to identify the cremains of the decedent.

In these days of heightened security, it is important to call the airline before departure and ask whether they have any special regulation or procedure regarding the transportation of human ashes.

SPOUSE — THE MILITARY BURIAL

Subject to availability of burial spaces, an honorably discharged veteran, his dependent child and his surviving spouse may be buried in the military cemeteries located in Oklahoma. There are two national cemeteries located within the state.

Fort Gibson National Cemetery (918) 478-2334
1423 Cemetery Road
Fort Gibson, OK 74434

Fort Sill National Cemetery (580) 492-3200
2648 N.E. Jake Dunn Road
Elgin, OK 73538

BURIAL AT ARLINGTON

An honorably discharged veteran can be buried in the national military cemetery at Arlington, Virginia. The Department of the Army is in charge of the Arlington National Cemetery. You can call the Interment Service Branch at (703) 607-8585 for information about having a veteran buried there.

Special Situation

THE COST OF A MILITARY BURIAL

Burial space in a National Cemetery is free of charge. Cemetery employees will open and close the grave and mark it with a headstone or grave marker without cost to the family. If requested, the local Veteran's Administration ("VA") will provide the family with a memorial flag. The VA will not pay to have the body transported to the cemetery, so the family needs to make arrangements with a funeral firm to transport the remains to the cemetery.

Regardless of where an honorably discharged veteran is buried, allowances may be available for the plot, and the burial and grave marker expenses. The amount varies depending on factors such as whether the veteran died because of a service related injury. The VA will not reimburse any burial or funeral expense for the spouse of a veteran. For information about reimbursement of funeral and burial expenses you can call the VA at (800) 827-1000.

The Department of Veteran's Affairs has a Web site with information on the following topics:

- National and Military Cemeteries
- Burial, Headstones and Markers
- State Cemetery Grants Program
- Obtaining Military Records
- Locating Veterans

VA CEMETERY WEB SITE
http://www.cem.va.gov

SPOUSE

BENEFITS FOR SPOUSE OF DECEASED VETERAN

The surviving spouse of an honorably discharged veteran should contact the Veteran's Administration to determine whether he/she is eligible for any benefits. For example, if the decedent had minor or disabled children, his spouse may also be eligible for a monthly benefit of Dependency and Indemnity Compensation ("DIC"). If the Veteran's surviving spouse receives nursing home care under Medicaid, then the spouse might be eligible for monthly payments from the VA.

Whether a surviving spouse is eligible for any of these benefits depends on many factors including whether the decedent was serving on active duty, whether his death was service related, and the surviving spouse's assets and income. DIC benefits are discontinued should the surviving spouse remarry; however, the law allows payments to be resumed in the event that the subsequent marriage ends because of death or divorce.

For information about whether the surviving spouse is eligible for any benefit related to the decedent's military service call the VA at (800) 827-1000. You can receive a printed statement of public policy: VA Pamphlet 051-000-00217-2 FEDERAL BENEFITS FOR VETERANS AND DEPENDENTS by sending a check in the amount of $5 to

THE SUPERINTENDENT OF DOCUMENTS
P.O. Box 371954
Pittsburgh, PA 15250-7954

Information is also available at the VA Web site.

VETERAN'S ADMINISTRATION
http://www.va.gov

☎ LAWYER THE WRONGFUL DEATH

It is important to have a Personal Injury attorney investigate any accidental death, to determine whether the death was caused by the wrongful act of a person, or company. If the accident was related to the decedent's job, the family may wish to consult with a Worker's Compensation attorney as well.

The Personal Representative has the right to bring a law suit on behalf of the decedent's Estate if his death was caused by the wrongful act of a person or company. If no Personal Representative is appointed, the law suit can be filed by the surviving spouse or if no spouse, by the next of kin (OS 12-1054).

Money awarded can be used to pay for the decedent's medical and burial expenses, legal expenses and costs. Whatever remains goes to his spouse, child, next of kin, in the same proportion as they are entitled to inherit his personal property. For example, if his surviving spouse is entitled to half of personal property, and his children the other half, then each get half the award (OS 12-1053(B)).

Up to $50,000 of a wrongful death award is free from the claims of the decedent's creditors. Anything over that value is available to pay his debts with the exception of *punitive damages*; i.e., monies that are warded by the Court to punish the wrong doer (OS 31-1(A)(21)).

Special Situation

VICTIMS OF CRIME COMPENSATION ACT

The State of Oklahoma reimburses crime victims or a dependent of a deceased victim who suffer loses not covered by insurance, public funds, or any other compensation. If the decedent died because of a criminal act, you may be eligible to be reimbursed for loses under the OKLAHOMA CRIME VICTIMS COMPENSATION ACT. Compensation can be awarded for funeral and burial expenses, medical expenses, psychological counseling, lost support, etc. Total compensation may not exceed $20,000 (OS 21-142.13(B)). To be eligible, the following must be true:

- The decedent was an innocent victim.
- The crime was reported to authorities within 72 hours of its discovery.
- There was full cooperation with law enforcement officers by the victim and/or his family.
- The claim for compensation was filed within one year from the injury or discovery of the body.

However, the Compensation Board may allow up to two years to file the claim if there is some good reason for the delay (OS 21-142.10).

You can obtain a claim form from the District Attorney's office or you can write to:

Crime Victims Compensation Board
Oklahoma District Attorneys Council
421 NW 13th St., Suite 290
Oklahoma City, OK 73106

You can download a claim form from the District Attorneys Council Web site.

VICTIM SERVICES DIVISION
http://www.odawan.net/victim

Special Situation

THE UNCLAIMED BODY

When an inmate of any state, county or municipal institution dies, the superintendent, or other person in charge, will notify the relative of the decedent. If, within 24 hours, no relative can be found, or if no one will take responsibility for the disposition of the body, the person in charge of the body will offer it to the State Anatomical Board for the purpose of education or research.

The same procedure is followed in the case of an indigent or unclaimed body. Police make every effort to identify and locate the family of an unclaimed body. If no one is willing to claim the body, it is offered to the State Anatomical Board.

The State Anatomical Board will hold the donated body for 30 days to determine whether anyone will come forward to claim the body (OS 63-94(A)).

At the end of 30 days, they will transfer the body to a school for research. If the body is not suitable for study, or if they do not need the body, the State Anatomical Board will notify the County Commissioners that the donation is declined. Upon such written notification, the Commissioners will arrange for burial at public expense (OS 63-92).

THE INDIGENT VETERAN

Honorably discharged veterans who are indigent, can be buried without charge. All the family need do is contact the VA as explained on page 18.

Special Situation

THE PROBLEM
FUNERAL OR BURIAL

The funeral and burial industry is well regulated by the state and federal government. Under Oklahoma law the acts subject to disciplinary action include:

- ☒ Failure to provide a price list at the beginning of the discussion, or failing to provide an itemized price list of the goods and services purchased at the end of the discussion.
- ☒ Delivering goods of a lesser quality than presented to the purchaser as a sample
- ☒ Using a false or misleading advertisement
- ☒ Paying kick-backs to generate business
- ☒ Selling a used casket without tell the customer that it was used as a rental casket (Oklahoma Administrative Code 235:10-7-2(13).

Funeral directors are licensed professionals so it is unusual to have a problem with the funeral or burial or cremation. If, however, you had a bad experience with any aspect of the funeral then you can file a complaint with the state licensing agency:

The Board of Embalmers and Funeral Directors
4545 N. Lincoln Blvd., Suite 175
Oklahoma City, OK 73103
Telephone (405) 522-1790

☎ **LAWYER**

In addition to filing a complaint with the Board, you may wish to consult with an attorney who is experienced in litigation matters to learn of other legal remedies available to you.

☎ LAWYER THE MISSING BODY

Few things are more difficult to deal with than a missing person. The emotional turmoil created by the "not knowing" is often more difficult than the finality of death. The legal problems created by the disappearance are also more difficult than if the person simply died. It may take a two-part legal process — the appointment of a ***Conservator*** to handle the missing person's affairs while he is missing, and a Probate proceeding after the Court has issued an order that the missing person is presumed to be dead.

APPOINTING A CONSERVATOR

An ***Absentee*** is a person who is missing and cannot be found after a diligent search. If the Absentee has business matters that need attending (bills that need to be paid, family to be supported, etc.), then once six months have passed, his next of kin can ask the Probate Court to appoint a Conservator. For soldiers missing in action, the family can ask the Court to appoint a Conservator three months after the Department of Defense declares him to be missing (OS 60-361).

BEGINNING THE PROBATE PROCEDURE

Anyone who has the right to inherit the Absentee's property can begin the Probate process any time there is sufficient evidence that the Absentee is dead, or after the Absentee has been missing for seven years. The judge will hear evidence to determine whether the missing person should be presumed dead; and if so, the Probate procedure can go forward (OS 58-946).

THE DEATH CERTIFICATE

It is the job of the funeral director to provide information about the decedent. He will complete his portion of the death certificate and submit it to the Local Registrar. The Local Registrar will complete his portion of the death certificate, make a copy of it and return it to the funeral director. Within 24 hours the director must take the certificate to the Court Clerk of the county where the death occurred. The funeral director will complete an application requesting certified copies of the death certificate.

It is important that the information you give to the funeral director is correct. You need to check the form to be sure names are correctly spelled and dates correctly written. Once the Local Registrar signs the death certificate, no change can be made except through State Registrar of Vital Statistics. It will be difficult and time consuming to make a correction once the death certificate is placed in the permanent file of the State Registrar (OS 63-1-307(3)).

The funeral director will order as many certified copies of the death certificate as you request. Most establishments require an original certified copy and not a photocopy so you need to order sufficient certified copies. The following is a list of institutions that may request a certified copy:

- Each insurance company that insured the decedent or his property (health, life, car insurance, etc.)
- Each financial institution in which the decedent had money invested (brokerage houses, banks)
- The decedent's pension fund
- Each credit card company used by the decedent
- The IRS and the Social Security Administration
- Tag Agency of the Oklahoma Tax Commission

Some airlines and car rental companies offer a discount for short notice, emergency trips. If you have family flying in for the funeral, you may wish to order a few extra copies of the death certificate so that they can obtain an airline or car rental discount.

Under Oklahoma law, death certificates are confidential records. Certified copies of the a death certificate are issued to the family's attorney and funeral director, or to a family member or beneficiary of the decedent's Estate (OS 63-1-323).

If you wish to order certified copies of the death certificate at a later date, you can ask your funeral director or your attorney to get a copy for you. If you are a member of the family or a beneficiary of the decedent you can write to:

VITAL RECORDS SERVICE
Oklahoma State Department Of Health
1000 Northeast 10th
Oklahoma City, OK 73117

You will need to explain your relationship to the decedent and why you wish a copy of the death certificate. You will need to provide them with roof of your identity. It is a good idea to first call them at (405) 271-4040 to check the cost and ask about what information they require.

VIA THE INTERNET

You can download an Application for death certificate from the Web site of the Oklahoma Department of Health.

OKLAHOMA DEPT. OF HEALTH
http://www.health.state.ok.us

About Probate

Once a person dies, all of the property he owns as of the date of his death is referred to as the ***decedent's Estate.*** If the decedent owned property that was in his name only (not jointly or in trust for someone) then some sort of court procedure may be necessary to determine who is entitled to ownership of the property. The name of the court procedure is ***Probate***. We will use the term "Court" or "Probate Court" to refer to the judge who is presiding over Probate matters.

The root of the word Probate is "to prove." It refers to the first job of the Probate Court, that is, to examine proof of whether the decedent left a valid Will. The second job of the Probate Court is to appoint someone to wrap up the affairs of the decedent by paying the cost of the Probate procedure, any outstanding bills, and then distributing whatever is left to the proper beneficiary. If the decedent left a valid Will naming someone as *Executor* of his Estate, then the Court will appoint that person for the job and issue *Letters Testamentary* giving him authority to administer the Estate. If the decedent died without a Will, then the Probate Court will appoint someone to be the *Administrator* of his Estate and issue *Letters of Administration.*

For simplicity we will refer to the person appointed by the court to settle the decedent's Estate as the ***Personal Representative***, and the document authorizing him to act, as ***Letters***.

There are different ways to conduct a Probate procedure depending on the value of the property that is being Probated, and whether the decedent owned real property at the time of his death. We will refer to the property that is distributed as part of a Probate proceeding as the decedent's ***Probate Estate*** and the method of conducting the Probate, as the ***Estate Administration***.

Chapter 6 explains the different kinds of Estate Administration that are available in the state of Oklahoma.

But we are getting ahead of ourselves. First we need to determine whether a Probate procedure is necessary. To answer that question we need to know exactly what the decedent owned, so the next two chapters explain how to identify, and then locate, the decedent's assets.

Giving Notice Of The Death 2

Those closest to the decedent usually notify family members and close friends by telephone. The funeral director will arrange to have an obituary published in as many different newspapers as the family requests, but there is still the job of notifying the government and people who were doing business with the decedent. That job is the duty of whoever is appointed as Personal Representative of the decedent's Estate.

Oklahoma law gives an order of priority for the appointment of Personal Representative. Whoever the decedent named as Executor or Personal Representative of his Will has top priority. Once appointed, it is his job to give notice of the death.

If the decedent died without a valid Will, the surviving spouse has priority to be appointed as Personal Representative, so the surviving spouse needs to let every one know of the death. If there is no spouse, the job falls to his next of kin. By ***next of kin,*** we mean those people who inherit the decedent's property according to Oklahoma's LAWS OF DESCENT AND DISTRIBUTION. Those laws are explained in Chapter 5.

The person who has the job of settling the decedent's Estate should begin to give notice as soon as is practicable after the death. Two government agencies that need to be notified are the Social Security Administration and the IRS. This chapter gives their telephone number as well as other agencies that need to be notified.

NOTIFYING SOCIAL SECURITY

Many funeral directors will, as part of their service package, notify the Social Security Administration of the death. You may wish to check to see that this has been done. You can do so by calling (800) 772-1213. If you are hearing impaired call (800) 325-0778 TTY. You will need to give the Social Security Administration the full legal name of the decedent as well as his Social Security number and date of birth.

Special Situation

DECEDENT RECEIVING SOCIAL SECURITY

If the decedent was receiving checks from Social Security, you need to determine whether his last check needs to be returned to the Social Security Administration. Each Social Security check is a payment for the prior month, provided that person lives for the entire prior month. If the decedent died on the last day of the month, you should not cash the check for that month.

For example, if he died on July 31st, you need to return the check that the Social Security mailed out in August. If however, he died on August 1st the check sent in August need not be returned because that check was payment for the month of July.

If the Social Security check is electronically deposited into a bank account, notify the bank and the Social Security Administration that the account holder died. If the check needs to be returned, the Social Security Administration will withdraw it electronically from the bank account. You will need to keep the account open until the funds are withdrawn.

SPOUSE

SPOUSE/CHILD'S SOCIAL SECURITY BENEFITS

If the decedent had sufficient work credits, the Social Security Administration will give the decedent's widow(er) or if unmarried, then the decedent's minor children, a one-time death benefit in the amount of $255.

SURVIVORS BENEFITS:

The spouse (or former spouse) of the decedent may be eligible for Survivors Benefits. Benefits vary depending on the amount of work credits earned by the decedent; whether the decedent had minor or disabled children; the spouse's age; how long they were married; etc. The minor child of the decedent may be eligible for benefits regardless of whether the child's father (the decedent) ever married the child's mother. Paternity can be established by any one of several methods including the father acknowledging his child in writing or verbally to members of his family. For more information you can call the Social Security Administration at (800) 772-1213.

SOCIAL SECURITY BENEFITS

A spouse or former spouse can collect social security benefits based on the decedent's work record. This value may be greater than the spouse now receives. It is important to make an appointment with your local Social Security office and determine whether you as the spouse (or former spouse) or parent of decedent's minor child are eligible for any Social Security or Survivor benefit. The Social Security Administration has a Web site from which you can down load publications that explain survivors benefits.

SOCIAL SECURITY ADMINISTRATION
http://www.ssa.gov

Special Situation

DECEDENT WITH GOVERNMENT PENSION

Any pension or annuity check received after the date of death of a federal retiree, or a survivor annuitant, needs to be returned to the U.S. Treasury. If the check is direct deposited to a bank account, call the financial institution and ask them to return the check. If the check is sent by mail, you need to return it to the return mail address on the Department of Treasury envelope in which the check was mailed. Include a letter explaining the reason for the return of the check and stating the decedent's date of death.

APPLY FOR BENEFITS

A survivor annuity may be available to a surviving spouse, and/or minor or disabled child. In some cases, a former spouse may be eligible for benefits. Even though you notify the government of the death, they will not automatically give you benefits to which you may be entitled. You need to apply for those benefits by notifying the Office of Personnel Management ("OPM") of the death and requesting that they send you an application for survivor benefits. You can call them at (888) 767-6738 or you can write to:

U. S. OFFICE OF PERSONNEL MANAGEMENT
RETIREMENT OPERATIONS CENTER
Post Office Box 45
Boyers, PA 16017-4500

You will find brochures and information about Survivor's Benefits at the OPM Web site.

U.S. OFFICE OF PERSONNEL MANAGEMENT
http://www.opm.gov

Special Situation

DECEDENT WITH COMPANY PENSION OR ANNUITY

In most cases, pension and annuity checks are payment for the prior month. If the decedent received his pension or annuity check before his death, then no monies need be returned. Pension checks and/or annuity checks received after the date of death may need to be returned to the company. You need to notify the company of the death to determine the status of the last check sent to the decedent.

Before notifying the company, locate the policy or pension statement that is the basis of the income. That document should tell whether there is a beneficiary of the pension or annuity funds now that the pensioner or annuitant is dead. If you cannot locate the document, use the return address on the check envelope and ask the company to send you a copy of the plan. Also request that they forward to you any claim form that may be required in order for the survivor or beneficiary to receive benefits under that pension plan or policy.

If the pension/annuity check is direct deposited to the decedent's account, then ask the bank to assist you in locating the company and notifying the company of the death.

Special Situation

DECEDENT WITH AN IRA or QUALIFIED RETIREMENT PLAN ("QRP")

Anyone who is a beneficiary of an Individual Retirement Account ("IRA") or QRP needs to keep in mind that income taxes may not have been paid on monies placed in an IRA or QRP account. In such case, significant taxes may be due when the money is withdrawn. You need to learn what options are available to you as a beneficiary of the plan and the tax consequences of each option. You will need to ask an accountant how much will be due in taxes for each option. Once you know all the facts, you will be able to make the best choice for your circumstance.

SPOUSE

There are special options available if the spouse is the beneficiary of the decedent's IRA account. The spouse has the right to withdraw the money from the account or roll it over into the spouse's own retirement account. Although the employer can explain options that are available, the spouse still needs to understand the tax consequence of choosing any given option. It is important to consult with an accountant to determine the best way to go.

If the decedent had a QRP, the plan may permit the spouse to roll the balance of the account into a new IRA. The spouse needs to contact the decedent's employer for an explanation of the plan and all the options that are available at this time.

NOTIFYING IRS

THE FINAL INCOME TAX RETURN

The surviving spouse can file a final joint income tax return. If there is no surviving spouse, it is the Personal Representative's job to file the decedent's final return. If no Probate procedure is necessary, whoever takes possession of the decedent's property needs to file the return.

In Oklahoma, everyone who earns $1,000 per year or more, must file an Oklahoma income tax return. Even those who live in another state must file an Oklahoma return if they earned $1,000 or more within the state. The decedent's final federal income tax return (IRS form 1040) needs to be filed by April 15th of the year following the year in which he died. The state income tax is filed at the same time (OS 68-2368(G)(1)). You can get information about filing the final Oklahoma return by calling the Taxpayer Assistance Division at (800) 522-8165 Extension 13160 or by visiting the Oklahoma Tax Commission Web site.

OKLAHOMA TAX COMMISSION
http://www.oktax.state.ok.us

You may want to keep the decedent's bank account open until you determine whether the decedent is entitled to an income tax refund. See Chapter 6 for an explanation of how to obtain a tax refund.

THE GOOD NEWS

Monies inherited from the decedent are generally not counted as income to you, so you do not pay federal income tax on those monies. If the monies you inherit later earn interest or income for you, then of course you will report that income as you do any other type of income.

Both the federal and state government have the right to impose an ***Estate Tax*** on property transferred to a beneficiary as a result of the death. All the property owned as of the date of death becomes the decedent's ***Taxable Estate.*** This includes *real property* (residential lots, condominiums etc.) and *personal property* (life insurance policies, cars, business interests, securities, IRA accounts, etc.). It includes property held in the decedent's name alone, as well as property that he held jointly or in Trust. It also includes gifts given by the decedent during his lifetime that exceeded $10,000 per person, per year. In the year 2002, the ***Annual Gift Tax Exclusion*** was adjusted for inflation to $11,000 (26 U.S.C. 2503).

For most of us, this is not a concern because no federal Estate Tax need be paid unless the decedent's Taxable Estate exceeds the federal ***Estate Tax Exclusion*** amount. That value is currently one and a half million dollars and is scheduled to go even higher:

YEAR	ESTATE TAX EXCLUSION AMOUNT
2005	$1,500,000
2006-2008	$2,000,000
2009	$3,500,000

Under current law, the federal Estate Tax is scheduled to be phased out in the year 2010, but reinstated once again in the year 2011 with an Exclusion Amount of $1,000,000 — unless lawmakers change the tax law once again.

There is an unlimited marital tax deduction for property transferred to the surviving spouse who is a U.S. citizen; so in most cases, no Estate tax need be paid if the decedent was married. Regardless of whether taxes are due, federal and state Estate tax returns must be filed whenever the decedent's Estate exceeds the federal Estate Tax Exclusion Amount in effect as of his date of death. Both state and federal returns are due within 9 months of the date of death.

THE OKLAHOMA ESTATE TAX

Oklahoma imposes its own Estate Tax on property transferred within the state because of the death. The state allows a ***Tax Exemption*** for property inherited by the decedent's parents, his *lineal descendants* (child, grandchild, great-grandchild, etc.), stepchildren or their lineal descendants. This Exemption is scheduled to increase in the year 2006:

YEAR	OKLAHOMA ESTATE TAX EXEMPTION
2005	$950,000
2006	$1,000,000

Transfers to anyone else is taxed at the rate of 1% for amounts less than $10,000, graduating up to 15% for amounts over one million dollars (OS 68-802, 68-803, 68-825).

The Oklahoma Estate Tax is called an "Add-on Tax" because in the event that the Oklahoma Estate Tax is less than the credit allowed by the federal Estate Tax, Oklahoma will impose an addition tax equal to the difference between the Oklahoma Estate Tax and the taxes that would have been paid to the federal government, had it not been for the federal Estate Tax Exclusion Amount (OS 68-804).

As with federal Estate Taxes, Oklahoma allows a spousal deduction, so, in general, there is no Estate Tax on property passing to the decedent's spouse. However, once the surviving spouse dies, all of his Estate is subject to Estate Taxes.

THE UN-UNIFIED GIFT TAX

Up until the year 2002, if you gave someone more than $10,000 in any given year you had to report that gift to the IRS. As explained, the Annual Gift Tax Exclusion is now adjusted for the cost of living, so now any gift in excess of $11,000 must be reported. The IRS keeps a running count of amounts you give to someone that exceed the Annual Gift Tax Exclusion. Although you are required to report amounts over the Annual Exclusion value, no tax is due unless that running total is more than the federal lifetime Gift Tax Exclusion amount. If your running total does not exceed that amount during your lifetime, once you die, the cumulative value of gifts reported to the IRS will be added to your Taxable Estate.

Up until the change in the tax law in 2001, the Gift and Estate Tax were unified. No Gift Tax needed to be paid unless the total value of the taxable gifts exceeded the federal Estate Tax Exclusion amount. That changed in 2004. In 2004, the federal Estate Tax Exclusion amount went up to $1,500,000, but the amount for the Gift Tax Exclusion remained at $1,000,000, so they are no longer unified.

To summarize:
If you make a gift to someone that is greater than the Annual Gift Tax Exclusion for that year, you must report the gift to the IRS. The IRS will keep count of values that you gave in excess of the Annual Gift Tax Exclusion. In 2004, and thereafter, if that sum exceeds $1,000,000, you will pay a Gift Tax on any amount you give that is over the Annual Gift Tax Exclusion. The Estate Tax is scheduled to be repealed in 2010, but not the Gift Tax.

Oklahoma does not have a Gift Tax at this time.

The current federal Estate tax is scheduled to be phased out in the year 2010, but a new Capital Gains Tax is scheduled for 2010 that may prove even more costly than the Estate Tax. The new Capital Gains Tax is related to the way inherited property is evaluated by the federal government. Real and personal property is inherited at a "step up" in basis, meaning that if the decedent's property has increased in value from the time he acquired it, the beneficiary will inherit the property at its fair market value as of the decedent's date of death. For example, if the decedent bought stock for $20,000 and it is worth $50,000 as of his date of death, the beneficiary will take a step-up in basis of $30,000; i.e. the beneficiary inherits the stock at the current $50,000 value. If the beneficiary sells the stock for $50,000, he pays no Capital Gains Tax. If the beneficiary holds onto the stock and later sells it for $60,000, the beneficiary will pay a Capital Gains Tax only on the $10,000 increase in value since the decedent's death.

Up to 2009, there is no limit to the amount a beneficiary can take as a step-up in basis. But in 2010 caps are set in place. The decedent's Estate will be allowed a 1.3 million dollar step-up in basis, plus another 3 million for property passing to the surviving spouse. The new law could result in significant Capital Gains Taxes that the beneficiary must pay. For example, suppose in 2010 you inherit a business from your father that he purchased for $100,000 and it is now worth 2 million dollars. There is a capital gain of 1.9 million dollars, but you are allowed a step-up in basis of only 1.3 million. If you sell it for 2 million dollars $600,000 of your inheritance will be subject to a Capital Gains Tax.

SPOUSE — SELLING THE HOME

In the tough "ole days" the IRS used to allow Capital Gains Tax Exclusion (up to $125,000) on the sale of one's ***homestead*** (the principal residence). A person had to be 55 or older to take advantage of the Exclusion, and it was a once-in-a-lifetime tax break. If a married couple sold their home and took the Tax Exclusion it was "used up" and no longer available to either partner.

In these, the good times, the IRS allows you to sell your home and up to $250,000 ($500,000 for a married couple) of the gain is free of the Capital Gains Tax. There is no limit to the number of times you can use the Exclusion, provided you own and live in the home as your primary residence at least two of the last five years prior to the sale (26 U.S.C. 121).

If, under the old law, the decedent and his spouse used their "once in a lifetime" Homestead Tax Exclusion, with this new law, the surviving spouse can sell the homestead and once again take advantage of a tax break.

Special Situation

BENEFICIARY OF THE DECEDENT'S HOMESTEAD

People who own and occupy real property as their primary residence in Oklahoma are entitled to a Homestead Tax Exemption of $1,000 of its assessed value. There is an additional Homestead Tax Exemption of $1,000 for the head of the household whose income from all sources for the previous year does not exceed $20,000 (OS 68-2890(A)).

There are Tax Credits available for those 65 or older, or totally disabled, and whose gross income for the year is not greater than $12,000. A claim for a Tax Credit needs to be submitted to the Oklahoma Tax Commission on or before June 30th for property taxes that were paid in the preceding year (OS 68-2905, 68-2906, 68-2908).

The County Assessor needs to be notified if the decedent's homestead is transferred to a new owner through a sale or inheritance. He will also assist you in applying for any Tax Exemption or Tax Credit that may be due to the decedent (OS 68-2890.1).

A new owner who intends to occupy the property as his homestead, needs to apply to the County Assessor for his own Homestead Tax Exemption and Tax Credit.

You can get information about Oklahoma property taxes from the Oklahoma Tax Commission Web site.

OKLAHOMA TAX COMMISSION
http://www.oktax.state.ok.us

Special Situation

DECEDENT WITH A TRUST

A decedent who was the ***Grantor*** (or *Settlor*) of a Trust, was probably managing the Trust as *Trustee* during his lifetime. The document that sets out the terms of the Trust (the ***Trust Agreement)*** should name a ***Successor Trustee*** to manage the Trust now that the Grantor is deceased. The Agreement may instruct the Successor Trustee to make certain gifts once the Grantor dies or the Trust document may direct the Successor Trustee to hold money in trust for a beneficiary of the Trust.

☎ LAWYER

IF YOU ARE SUCCESSOR TRUSTEE

If you are the Successor Trustee, then in addition to following the terms of the Trust, you are required to obey all of the laws of the state of Oklahoma relating to the administration of the Trust. You should consult with an attorney experienced in Estate Planning to help you administer the Trust according to the law and without any liability to yourself.

IF YOU ARE A BENEFICIARY OF THE TRUST

If you are a beneficiary of the Trust, you need to get a copy of the Trust to learn how the Trust will be administered now that the Grantor or Settlor is deceased. Most Trust documents are written in "legalese," so you may want to employ your own attorney to review the Trust, and to explain your rights under the Trust.

NOTIFYING THE BUSINESS COMMUNITY

People and companies who were doing business with the decedent need to be notified of his death. This includes utility companies, credit card companies, banks, brokerage firms and any company that insured the decedent.

NOTIFY CREDIT CARD COMPANIES

You need to notify the decedent's credit card companies of the death. If you can find the contract with the credit card company, check to see whether the decedent had credit card insurance. If the decedent had credit card insurance, then the balance of the account is now paid in full. If you cannot find the contract, contact the company and get a copy of the contract along with a statement of the balance due as of the date of death.

DESTROY DECEDENT'S CREDIT CARDS

You need to destroy all of the decedent's credit cards. If you hold a credit card jointly with the decedent, then it is important to waste no time in closing that account and opening another in your name only.

That's something Barbara knows from hard experience. She and Hank never married but they did live together for several years before he died from liver disease. Hank came from a well to do family so he had enough money to support himself and Barbara during his long illness. Hank put Barbara on all of his credit card accounts so that she could purchase things when he became too ill to go shopping with her. After the funeral, Barbara had a gathering of friends and family at their apartment. Barbara was so preoccupied with her loss that she never noticed that Hank's credit cards were missing until the bills started coming in.

Barbara did not know who ran up the bills on Hank's credit cards during the month following his death. It was obvious that Hank's signature had been forged — but who forged it? One credit card company suspected that it might have been Barbara herself to get out of paying the bill by saying that the card had been stolen

Because the cards were held jointly, Barbara became liable to either pay the charges to the credit card or to prove that she did not make the purchases. She was able to clear her credit record but it took several months and she had to employ an attorney to help her do so.

NOTIFY INSURANCE COMPANIES

Examine the decedent's financial records to determine the name and telephone number of all of the companies that insured the decedent or his property. This includes real property insurance, motor vehicle insurance, health insurance and life insurance.

MOTOR VEHICLE INSURANCE

Locate the insurance policy for any type of motor vehicle owed by the decedent (car, truck, boat, airplane) and notify the insurance company of the death. Determine how long insurance coverage continues after the death. Ask the insurance agent to explain what things are covered under the policy. Is the motor vehicle covered for all types of casualty (theft, accident, vandalism, etc.) or is coverage limited in some way?

If you can continue coverage, then determine when the next insurance payment is due. Hopefully, the car will be sold or transferred to a beneficiary before that date, but if not, you need to arrange for sufficient insurance coverage during the Probate procedure.

Special Situation

ACCIDENTAL DEATH

If the decedent died as a result of an accident, then check for all possible sources of accident insurance coverage including his homeowner's policy. Some credit card companies provide accident insurance as part of their contract with their card holders. If the decedent died in an automobile accident, check to see whether he was covered by any type of travel insurance, such as rental car insurance. If he belonged to an automobile club, such as AAA, then check whether he had accident insurance as part of his club membership.

LIFE INSURANCE COMPANIES

If the decedent's life was insured, you need to locate the policy and notify the company of his death. Call each life insurance company and ask what they require in order to forward the insurance proceeds to the beneficiary. Most companies will ask you to send them the original policy and a certified copy of the death certificate. Send the original policy by certified mail or any of the overnight services that require a signed receipt for the package. Make a copy of the original policy for your records before mailing the original policy to the company.

BANK ACCOUNT LIFE INSURANCE

Many banks, credit unions, savings and loan associations provide life insurance at no cost to the primary owner of the account. While the amounts are generally small ($1,000 to $5,000), it is insurance that is often overlooked when settling the decedent's affairs. If you do not find a record of such policy, contact each financial institution to determine whether such insurance is provided by the company.

IF YOU CANNOT LOCATE THE POLICY

If you know that the decedent was insured, but you cannot locate the insurance policy, you can contact the company and request a copy of the policy. A tougher question is how to locate the policy if you do not know the name of the insurance company. The American Council of Life Insurers offers suggestions that you may find helpful at the Missing Policy Inquiry page of their Web site.

AMERICAN COUNCIL OF LIFE INSURERS
http://www.acli.com

IF YOU CANNOT LOCATE THE COMPANY

If you cannot locate the insurance company it may be doing business under another name or it may no longer be doing business in the state of Oklahoma. Each state has abranch of government that regulates insurance companies doing business in that state. If you are having difficulty locating the insurance company you can call the Department of Insurance in the state where the policy was purchased and ask for assistance in locating the company. In Oklahoma you can call the Oklahoma Insurance Department at (405) 521-3966.

EAGLE PUBLISHING COMPANY OF BOCA has the telephone number of the Department of Insurance for each state at the PUBLIC INFORMATION section of its Web site.
http://www.eaglepublishing.com

WORK RELATED INSURANCE

If the decedent was employed, check his records for information about work related benefits. He may have survivor benefits from a company or group life insurance plan and/or a retirement plan. Also check with the employer about company benefits. If the decedent belonged to a union, contact them to determine whether there are any union benefits.

The decedent may have belonged to a professional, fraternal or social organization such as the local Chamber of Commerce, a Veteran's organization, the Kiwanis, AARP, the Rotary Club, etc. If he belonged to any such organization check to see whether the organization provided any type of insurance coverage.

Special Situation BUSINESS OWNED BY DECEDENT

If the decedent owned his own company or was a partner in a company he may have purchased "key man" insurance. Key man insurance is a policy designed to protect the company should a valuable employee become disabled or die. Benefits are paid to the company to compensate the company for the loss of someone who is essential to the continuation of the business. Ultimately the policy benefits those who inherit the business.

If the decedent had an ownership interest in an ongoing business (sole proprietor, shareholder or partner) there may be a shareholder's or partnership agreement requiring the company to purchase the decedent's share of the business. The Personal Representative or his attorney needs to investigate to see if there was a key man insurance policy and/or such purchase agreement.

Special Situation

CORPORATE OWNER OR REGISTERED AGENT

If the decedent was the sole owner of a corporation and the company stock was in his name only, then there may need to be a Probate procedure before the company can be transferred to the new owner.

Oklahoma statute requires each corporation to continuously maintain a Registered Agent in this state. If the decedent was the sole officer or Registered Agent of the company, the Secretary of State needs to be notified of the identity of the new officers and Registered Agent within 30 days (OS 18-1022(A)).

Forms to change officers or Registered Agent can be obtained by calling (405) 521-3912 by writing to:

BUSINESS FILING DEPARTMENT
2300 N. Lincoln Blvd., Room 101
Oklahoma City, OK 73105-4897

or you can download the form from the Internet.

OKLAHOMA SECRETARY OF STATE
http://www.sos.state.ok.us

If you were not actively involved in running the business, you might want to call the Secretary of State for information about the company (names, addresses of officers and directors, number of company shares, whether fees are current, etc.). You can also get that information by going to the Business Filing Department of the above Web site and then to the Business Records section.

HOMEOWNER'S INSURANCE

If the decedent owned his own home, then check whether there is sufficient insurance coverage on the property. The decedent may have neglected to increase his home insurance as the property appreciated in value. If you think the property may be vacant for some period of time, it is important to have vandalism coverage included in the policy. Once the property is sold, or transferred to the proper beneficiary, you can have the policy discontinued or transferred to the new owner. The decedent's Estate should receive a refund for the unused portion of the premium.

MORTGAGE INSURANCE

If the decedent had a mortgage on any parcel of real estate that he owned, he might have arranged with his lender for an insurance policy that pays off the mortgage balance in the event of his death. Look at the closing statement to see whether there was a charge for mortgage insurance. Also check with the lender to determine if such a policy was purchased.

If there was no mortgage insurance, and the decedent was the sole owner, the beneficiary of the property needs to make arrangements with the lender to continue making payments on the mortgage or to refinance the loan.

NOTIFY THE HOMEOWNER'S ASSOCIATION

If the decedent owned a condominium or a residence regulated by a homeowner's association, the association will need to be notified of the change of ownership. Once the property is transferred, the new owner will need to contact the association to learn of the rules and regulations of the association. The new owner will need to arrange to have notices of dues and assessments forwarded to him.

HEALTH INSURANCE

The Health Insurance carrier probably knows of the death, but it is a good idea to contact them to determine what coverage the decedent had under that insurance plan. If you cannot find the original policy, have the insurance company send you a copy of the policy so that you can determine whether medical treatment given to the decedent before his death was covered by that policy.

Special Situation

DECEDENT ON MEDICARE

If the decedent was covered by Medicare, you do not need to notify anyone, but you do need to know what things were covered by Medicare so that you can determine what medical bills are (or are not) covered by Medicare. The government publication MEDICARE AND YOU (Publication No. CMS-10050) explains what things are covered under Medicare and the different kinds of plans that are currently available. You can get the publication by writing to:

U.S. Dept. of Health and Human Services
Centers for Medicare and Medicaid Services
7500 Security Boulevard
Baltimore, MD 21244-1850

You can download the publication from the Internet.

MEDICARE WEB SITE
http://www.medicare.gov

The publication is available on Audiotape, in Braille, in large print and in Spanish. To receive a copy you can call (800) 633-4227. TTY users call (877) 486-2048.

SPOUSE — THE SPOUSE'S HEALTH INSURANCE

If the spouse of the decedent is insured under Medicare, then the death does not affect the surviving spouse's coverage. If the spouse was not covered by Medicare but has her own health insurance that also covered the decedent, then the spouse needs to notify the employer of the death because this may affect the cost of the plan to the employer and/or the spouse. If the spouse was covered under the decedent's policy then he/she needs to arrange for new coverage. There are federal laws that ensure continued coverage under the decedent's policy for a period of time depending on whether the decedent's employer falls under federal regulation.

If the decedent was employed by a federally regulated company (usually a company with at least twenty employees), under the Consolidated Omnibus Budget Reconciliation Act ("COBRA") the employer must make the company health plan available to the surviving spouse and any dependent child of the decedent for at least 36 months.

The employer is required to give notice to the surviving spouse that the spouse and/or dependent child have the right to continue coverage under the decedent's health plan. The spouse and/or child have 60 days from the date of death or 60 days after the employer sends notice (whichever is later) to tell the employer whether the surviving spouse and child wish to continue with the health insurance plan (29 U.S.C. 1162, 1163, 1165).

SPOUSE'S HEALTH INSURANCE (continued)

The only problem with continued coverage may be the cost. Before the death, the employer may have been paying some percentage of the premium. The employer has no such duty after the death unless there was some employment agreement stating otherwise. Under COBRA, the employer may charge the spouse for the full cost of the plan plus a 2% administrative fee.

If you have a question about your coverage under COBRA, you can call the U.S. Department of Labor ("DOL") at (800) 998-7542 and ask for the number of your local DOL office. You can also ask that they send you their publication HEALTH BENEFITS UNDER COBRA; or you can visit their Web site for more information.

U.S. DEPARTMENT OF LABOR
http://www.dol.gov/dol/pwba

NOTIFY ADVERTISERS

Probably the last one in the world to learn of the decedent's death is the direct mail advertiser. Advertisers are nothing if not tenacious. It is not uncommon for advertisements to be mailed to the decedent for more than ten years after the death. It is not because the advertiser is trying to sell something to the decedent, but rather the people who prepare (and sell) mailing lists do not know that the person is dead.

Those who sell mailing lists may not be motivated to update the list because of the cost of doing the necessary research; and perhaps because the price of the mailing list is often based on the number of people on the list. Even those who compose their own list may decide it is less costly to mail to everyone, than take the time (and money) to update the list.

If it gives you pleasure to think of advertisers spending substantial sums for nothing, then that is what you should do (nothing). But for those of you who wince each time you see another piece of mail addressed to the decedent, you can write to the Direct Marketing Association and ask that the name be deleted from all mailing lists:

Mail Preference Service
Direct Marketing Association
P.O. Box 9008
Farmingdale, NY 11735

You will need to give them the decedent's complete address, including zip code and every name variation that the decedent may have used; for example:

Theodore James Jones	T. J. Jones
Ted Jones	Ted J. Jones
T. James Jones	Jim Jones, etc.

✍ CHANGE BENEFICIARIES ✍

If the decedent was someone you named as beneficiary of your insurance policy, Will, Trust, brokerage account or pension plan, then you may need to name another beneficiary in his place:

INSURANCE POLICY ✍

If you named the decedent as the primary beneficiary of your life insurance policy, check to see whether you named a contingent (alternate) beneficiary in the event that the decedent did not survive you. If not, you need to contact the insurance company and name a new beneficiary. If you did name a contingent beneficiary, that person is now your primary beneficiary and you need to consider whether you wish to name a new contingent beneficiary.

HEALTH INSURANCE POLICY ✍

If the decedent was covered under your health insurance policy, your employer and the health insurer need to be notified of the death because this may affect the cost of the plan to you and/or your employer.

WILL OR TRUST ✍

Most Wills provide for a contingent beneficiary in the event that the person named as beneficiary dies first. If you named the decedent as your beneficiary, check to see whether you named an alternate beneficiary. If not, you need to have your attorney revise your Will and name a new beneficiary.

Similarly, if you are the Grantor or Settlor of a Trust and the decedent was one of the beneficiaries of your Trust, check the Trust document to see if you named an alternate beneficiary. If not, contact your attorney to prepare an amendment to the Trust, naming a new beneficiary.

BANK AND SECURITIES ACCOUNTS ✍

If the decedent was a beneficiary or joint owner of your bank or securities account, you may wish to arrange for a new beneficiary or joint owner at this time.

PENSION PLANS ✍

If the decedent was a beneficiary under your pension plan, you need to notify them of his death and name a new beneficiary. Many pension plans require that you notify them within a set period of time (usually 30 days) so it is important to notify them as soon as you are able. If the decedent was a beneficiary of your Individual Retirement Account ("IRA") or of your Qualified Retirement Plan ("QRP") and you did not provide for an alternate beneficiary, you need to name another beneficiary.

Before you choose an alternate beneficiary, it is important that you understand all of the options available to you. Not an easy task. There are many complex government regulations relating to IRA and QRP accounts. Even if you believe you understood your options when you set up your account, the federal government often changes those options.

Your choice of beneficiary might impact the amount of money you can withdraw each month, so it is important to consult with your accountant, tax attorney or financial planner, before you make your election.

NOTIFYING CREDITORS

It is the job of the person appointed as Personal Representative to notify the decedent's creditors of the death so that the creditor is given an opportunity to come forward and file a ***claim*** (a written demand for payment) for monies owed. The attorney for the Personal Representative usually takes care of the notice procedure. We will explain that procedure later in this book.

If no Probate proceeding is necessary, the next of kin can notify the creditors of the death, but before doing so, it is important to read Chapter 4: WHAT BILLS NEED TO BE PAID? That chapter explains what bills need to be paid and who is responsible to pay them.

Before any bill can be paid, you need to know whether the decedent left any asset that can be used to pay those debts. The next chapter explains how to identify, and then locate all of the property owned by the decedent.

Locating the Assets 3

It is important to locate the financial records of the decedent and then carefully examine those records. Even the partner of a long-term marriage should conduct a thorough search because the surviving spouse may be unaware of all that was owned (or owed) by the decedent.

It is not unusual for a surviving spouse to be surprised when learning of the decedent's business transactions, especially in those cases where the decedent had control of family finances. One such example is that of Sam and Henrietta. They married just as soon as Sam was discharged from the army after World War II. During their marriage, Sam handled all of the finances giving Henrietta just enough money to run the household.

Every now and again Henrietta would think of getting a job. She longed to have her own source of income and some economic independence. Each time she brought up the subject Sam would loudly object. He had no patience for this new "woman's lib" thing. Sam said he got married to have a real wife — one who would cook his meals and keep house for him.

Henrietta was not the arguing type. She rationalized, saying that Sam had a delicate stomach and dust allergies. He needed her to prepare his special meals and keep an immaculate house for him. Besides, Sam had a good job with a major cruise line and he needed her to accompany him on his frequent business trips.

Once Sam retired, he was even more cautious in his spending habits. Henrietta seldom complained. She assumed the reason for his "thrift" was that they had little money and had to live on his pension.

They were married 52 years when Sam died at the age of 83. Henrietta was 81 at the time of his death. She was one very happy, very angry and very aged widow when she discovered that Sam left her with assets worth well over a million dollars!

LOCATING RECORDS

As you go through the papers of the decedent you may come across documents that indicate property ownership, such as bank registers, stock or bond certificates, insurance policies, pension or annuity records, etc. Place all evidence of ownership in a single place. You will need to contact the different companies in order to transfer title to the proper beneficiary.

To obtain the property, you may need to produce evidence of the decedent's personal relationships, such as a marriage or birth certificate, or naturalization papers, or military personnel records. If you cannot locate the decedent's marriage or birth certificate, you can get a copy of those records from the Vital Records office in the state where the event took place. Many states (including Oklahoma) restrict access to these records to close family members or to the decedent's Personal Representative (OS 63-1-323(A)). See chapter 1 for the telephone number of the Vital Records office. You can use the Internet to locate the Vital Records office in other states by using your favorite search engine to find Vital Statistics or Vital Records.

You can obtain a copy of the military record of a deceased veteran by writing to:

The National Personnel Records Center
Military Personnel Records
9700 Page Avenue
St. Louis, MO 63132-5100

They will send you form SF 180 to complete. You can get the form from the Internet at http://www.cem.va.gov or from the National Archives and Records Administration Fax-On-Demand system. Dial (301) 713-6905 and request document number 2255.

COLLECT AND IDENTIFY KEYS

The decedent may have kept his records in a safe deposit box, so you may find that your first job is to locate the keys to the box. As you go through the personal effects of the decedent, collect and identify all the keys that you find. If you come across an unidentified key, it could be a key to a post office box (private or federal) or a safe deposit box located in a bank or in a private vault company. You will need to determine whether that key opens a box that contains property belonging to the decedent or whether the key is to a box no longer in use. Some ways to investigate are as follows:

☑ CHECK BUSINESS RECORDS

If the decedent kept receipts, look through those items to see if he paid for the rental of a post office or safe deposit box. Also, look at his check register to see if he wrote a check to the Postmaster or to any safe deposit or vault company. Look at his bank statements to see if there is any bank charge for a safe deposit box. Some banks bill separately for safe deposit boxes so check with all of the banks in which the decedent had an account to determine if he had a safe deposit box with that bank.

☑ CHECK THE KEY TYPE

If you cannot identify the key, then take it to each local locksmith and ask whether anyone can identify the type of facility that uses such keys. If that doesn't work, go to each bank, post office and private safe deposit box company where the decedent shopped, worked or frequented and ask whether they use the type of key that you found.

☑ CHECK THE MAIL

Check the mail over the next several months to see if the decedent receives a statement requesting payment for the next year's rental of a post office or safe deposit box.

You may find evidence of a brokerage account, bank account, or safe deposit box by examining correspondence addressed to the decedent. If the decedent was living alone, have his mail forwarded to the person he named as Personal Representative or Executor of his Will. If the decedent did not leave a Will, and no Probate procedure is necessary, the mail should be forwarded to his next of kin. Call the Postmaster and ask him to send you the necessary forms to make the change. Request that the mail be forwarded for the longest period allowed by law (currently one year).

The decedent may have been renting a post office box at his local post office branch or perhaps at the branch closest to where he did his banking. Ask the Postmaster to help you determine whether the decedent was renting a post office box. If so, then you need to locate the key to the box so that you can collect the decedent's mail.

Special Situation

LOST POST OFFICE BOX KEY

If the decedent had a post office box and you cannot locate it, contact the local postmaster and ask him what documentation is needed for you to get possession of the mail in that box. As before, you will ask the Postmaster to have all future mail addressed to that box, forwarded to the Personal Representative, or if no Probate is necessary, to the decedent's next of kin.

WHAT TO DO WITH CHECKS

You may receive checks in the mail made out to the decedent. Social Security checks, pension checks and annuity checks issued after the date of death may need to be returned to the sender. See pages 30 and 32 of this book. Other checks need to be deposited. If a Probate procedure is necessary, the Personal Representative will open a Probate Estate account and will deposit the decedent's checks to that account.

If no Probate procedure is necessary, checks can be deposited to any account held in the name of the decedent. The decedent is not here to endorse the check, but you can deposit it to his account by writing his bank account number on the back of the check and printing beneath it FOR DEPOSIT ONLY.

The bank will accept such an endorsement and deposit the check into the decedent's account. If the check is significant in value or the decedent had different accounts that are accessible to different people, then there needs to be cooperation and a sense of fair play. If not, the dollar gain may not nearly offset the emotional turmoil.

Such was the case with Gail. Her father made her a joint owner of his checking account to assist in paying his bills. He had macular degeneration and it was increasingly difficult for him to see. The father also had a savings account that was in his name only.

Gail's brother Ken had a good paying job in Alaska. Even though he lived at a distance, Ken, his wife and two children always spent the Christmas holidays with his father and sister.

Each summer, their father enjoyed leaving the heat of a Oklahoma to spend a few weeks in the cool Alaskan climate.

One summer, the father purchased a round trip ticket to Alaska. It cost several hundred dollars. Just before the departure date, the father had a heart attack and died. Gail called the airline to cancel the ticket. They refunded the money in a check made out to her father. She deposited the check to the joint account, and then closed it out.

As part of the Probate procedure, the money in the father's savings account was divided equally between Ken and his sister. Ken wondered what happened to the money from the airline tickets.

Gail explained "Dad paid for the tickets from the joint account, so I deposited the money back to that account. "

"Aren't you going to give me half?"

"Dad meant for me to have whatever was in that joint account. If he wanted you to have half of the money, he would have made you joint owner as well."

Ken didn't see it that way "That refund was part of Dad's Estate. It should have been deposited to his savings account to be divided equally between us. Are you going to force me to argue this in Court?"

Gail finally agreed to split the money with Ken, but the damage was done.

Gail complains that holidays are lonely since Dad died.

LOCATE FINANCIAL RECORDS

To locate the decedent's assets you need to find evidence of what he owned and where those assets are located. His financial records should lead you to the location of all of his assets, so your first job is to locate those records. The best place to start the search is in the decedent's home. Many people keep their financial records in a single place but it is important to check the entire house to be sure you did not miss something.

CHECK THE COMPUTER

Don't overlook that computer sitting silently in the corner. It may hold the decedent's check register and all of his financial records. You may want to monitor his E-mail for E-bank or on-line credit card accounts.

The computer may be programmed to protect this information. If you cannot access the decedent's financial records, you may need to employ a computer technician or computer consultant who will be able to print out all of the information on the hard drive of the computer. You can find such a technician or consultant by looking in the telephone book under COMPUTER SUPPORT SERVICES or COMPUTER SYSTEM DESIGNS & CONSULTANTS.

LOCATE TITLE TO WATERCRAFT

The Oklahoma Tax Commission is in charge of the titling and registration of all vessels and outboard motors in excess of 10 horsepower (OS 63-4003(B)(1)). If the Title Certificate is lost, the Personal Representative can apply for a duplicate at the Motor Vehicle Division, or at any Motor License Agency i.e., Tag Agency. See Chapter 6 for an explanation of how to transfer title to the watercraft.

LOCATE TITLE TO MOTOR VEHICLE

You should be able to locate the title to the decedent's motor vehicle. If not, you can obtain a duplicate title from the Oklahoma Tax Commission. You can call them at (405) 521- 3221 for information about what is needed in order to issue a duplicate title or go to the nearest Tag Agency. They can issue a replacement (duplicate) title to you. The Tag Agent will require proof of your authority to get a copy of the Title. In some cases, they will issue the replacement title only to the Personal Representative. It is a good idea to first call the Tag Agency and ask what information they require and the cost of obtaining the replacement Title. If you find there is a loan on the car, contact the lienholder and get a copy of the contract that is the basis of the loan.

THE LEASED CAR

You may find that the car is leased and not owned by the decedent. If so, contact the lessor and get a copy of the lease agreement. Check to see whether the decedent had life insurance as part of the agreement. If he did, then the lease may now be paid in full and the beneficiary of the car should be able to use the car for the remainder of the leasing period, or take title to the car, whichever option is available under the lease agreement.

The Personal Representative (or the beneficiary) can send the death certificate to the leasing company with a copy of the contract and a letter requesting that the transfer be made. If the lease is not paid in full upon the decedent's death, arrangements need to be made to satisfy the terms of the agreement. See Chapter 6 for information about transferring a leased car.

LOCATE TITLE TO MOBILE HOME

In Oklahoma, mobile homes are titled and registered in the same manner as a motor vehicle (OS 47-1113). If the decedent owned a parcel of land and his mobile home was permanently attached to that land, then turn to Chapter 6 for information about transferring the land and the mobile home to the proper beneficiary. If the mobile home is kept in a leased space, you need to locate the lease to the mobile home lot. If you cannot locate the lease, then contact the landlord for a copy, and proceed in the same manner as for a residential lease. See the next page.

LOCATE TITLE TO AIRCRAFT

If the decedent owned an aircraft, then you should find a certificate of title to the aircraft. The Civil Aviation Registry of the Federal Aviation Administration ("FAA") contains all of the ownership and security documents that have been filed with the FAA. If you cannot locate title to the aircraft you can contact the Civil Aviation Registry. They do not perform title searches, however they can give you a list of title search companies. If you wish to perform the title search yourself you can call the Aircraft Registration Branch at (405) 954-3116 for more information or you can visit the FAA Web site.

THE FEDERAL AVIATION ADMINISTRATION
http://www2.faa.gov

In addition to locating the title you need to find the registration to the aircraft. Oklahoma statute requires that all aircraft be registered with the Oklahoma Tax Commission. If you cannot locate the registration to the aircraft, contact the local Tag Agency to obtain a duplicate registration (OS 3-255(A)).

Special Situation

DECEDENT'S RESIDENTIAL LEASE

If the decedent was renting his residence, he may have a written lease agreement. It is important to locate the lease because the decedent's Estate may be responsible for payments under the lease. If you cannot find a lease, ask the landlord for a copy. If he reports that there was no written lease, verify that the decedent was on a month to month basis and then work out a mutually agreeable time in which to vacate the premises.

If a written lease is in effect, determine the end of the lease period, and whether the landlord is holding a security deposit. Ask whether he will agree to cancel the lease on condition that the property is promptly vacated and left in good condition. If the landlord wants to hold the Estate responsible to pay the balance of the lease, have your attorney review the lease to determine what rights and responsibilities remain now that the tenant is deceased.

☎ LAWYER

DECEDENT'S ONGOING BUSINESS

If the decedent was the sole owner of a business, or if he owned a partnership interest in a business, the Personal Representative needs to take possession of the decedent's business records and make arrangements for the operation of the business. The company accountant or company lawyer may be able to assist in obtaining the records. If you are a beneficiary of the Estate, consider consulting with your own attorney to determine what rights and responsibilities you may have in the business.

COLLECT DEEDS

Collect deeds to all of the property owned by the decedent. In addition to the deed, look for other documents associated with the property, such as a mortgage. You may come across a title insurance policy. The new owner might be able to turn in that policy and receive a discount toward the purchase of a new title insurance, so it is important to keep the policy together with the deed.

Instead of a title insurance policy you may find an ***Abstract of Title***. An Abstract of Title is a summary of the documents or facts appearing on the public record which affect title to the property. The Abstract will need to be updated once the property is transferred. We will discuss the transfer of property in Chapter 6.

Many people keep deeds in a safe deposit box. If you cannot find the deed in the decedent's home, then you need to determine whether he had a safe deposit box and if so, you need to examine the contents of the box. See the end of this chapter for information about how to access the decedent's safe deposit box.

If you know that the decedent owned real property (lot, residential property, condominium) but you cannot find the deed, then contact the recording department in the county where the property is located. In Oklahoma the County Clerk is in charge of recording. The Clerk can provide you with a copy of the last recorded deed. You might want to first call the Clerk to determine how to obtain a copy of the deed.

Special Situation

LOCATING THE OUT OF STATE DEED

You need to locate the deed and any related document (Abstract of Title, title insurance policy, recorded condominium approval, etc.) to out of state property owned by the decedent.

THE LOST OUT OF STATE DEED

If you know the decedent owned out of state real property, but cannot find the deed, you can use the same procedure just described, namely, you can check with the recording department in the county where the property is located. In some states the Clerk of the Circuit Court is in charge of the recording department. In other states it may be the County Recorder or Registrar of Deeds. The Clerk in the recording department should be able to give you a copy of the last recorded deed.

Many states index the property by the name of the current owner of the property, so if you know the county where the property is located, you should be able to find the deed by giving the decedent's name to the Clerk.

If you do not know the county in which the property is located, you will need to wait for the next tax bill. In many states the tax bill contains its legal description, or tax identification number.

COLLECT TAX RECORDS

The decedent's final state and federal income tax returns need to be filed so you should locate all of his tax records for the past three years. If you cannot locate his prior tax records, check his personal telephone book and/or his personal bank register to see if he employed someone to prepare his taxes. If you can locate his tax preparer, then he should have a copy of those records.

If you are unable to locate the decedent's federal tax returns, they can be obtained from the IRS. The IRS will send copies of the decedent's tax filings to anyone who has a *fiduciary relationship* with the decedent. The IRS considers the following people to be a fiduciary:

- the person appointed as the Personal Representative of the decedent's Estate
- the Successor Trustee of the decedent's Trust
- if the person died without a Will, whoever is legally entitled to possession of the decedent's property (See Chapter 5 for an explanation of the Laws of Descent).

The fiduciary can receive copies of the decedent's tax filings by notifying IRS that he/she is acting in a fiduciary capacity, and then requesting the copies.

To notify the IRS of the fiduciary capacity file Form 56:
NOTICE CONCERNING FIDUCIARY RELATIONSHIP

Your accountant can file these forms for you or you can obtain the forms from the IRS by calling (800) 829-3676 or you can download them from the FORMS section of the IRS Web site.

INTERNAL REVENUE SERVICE
http://www.irs.gov

LOCATE STATE INCOME TAX RETURN

Anyone who earns a net income of $1,000 or more is required to file a state income tax return. The decedent's surviving spouse can file a joint return. If there is no surviving spouse, the Personal Representative can do so. If no Probate is necessary, whoever is entitled to possession of the decedent's property will need to file the state income tax return at the same time the federal income tax return is filed (OS 68-2368).

You may need last year's return to help prepare the final return. If you cannot locate the decedent's state income tax returns you can get a copies from the OKLAHOMA TAX COMMISSION by calling Taxpayer Assistance Division at (800) 522-8165 Extension 13160.

LOCATE OUT OF STATE ACCOUNTS

If the decedent had out of state bank or brokerage accounts, then you might be able to locate them if they mail out monthly or quarterly statements. Not all financial institutions do so, but all institutions are required to send out an IRS tax form 1099 each year giving the amount of interest earned on that account. Once the forms come in, you will learn the location of all of the decedent's active accounts.

If the decedent was forgetful, he may have money in a lost bank account or abandoned safe deposit box. Property that is unclaimed is turned over to the Oklahoma State Treasurer after a period of time as set by Oklahoma law. The time period depends on the item:.

- 5 years after monies are payable under a life insurance policy or annuity or 2 years after the insured would have reached the limiting age as set by the policy's mortality table (OS 60-653(a)).
- 5 years for a gift certificate, Certificate of Deposit or last bank transaction (OS 60-651.2, 60-652).
- 15 years from the date of issue of a travelers check or money order (OS 60-651.1(a))

Before turning the property over to the state, the holder of the unclaimed property must try to contact the owner and return the property to him (OS 60-661). Once the property is turned over to the State Treasurer, he will publish a notice for two consecutive weeks in a newspaper of general circulation giving the name and address of the owner of the property (OS 60-662(A)).

You can determine whether there is a record identifying the decedent as the owner of unclaimed property by calling (405) 521-3191 or by writing to:

Oklahoma State Treasurer, Unclaimed Property Division
4545 N. Lincoln Blvd. Suite 106
Oklahoma City, OK 73105-3413

You can search for unclaimed property by going to the State Treasurer's Web site.

OKLAHOMA STATE TREASURER
http://www.treasurer.state.ok.us

CLAIMS IN OTHER STATES

Each state has an agency or department that is responsible for handling lost, abandoned or unclaimed property located within that state. If the decedent had residences in other states, then call the UNCLAIMED PROPERTY department of the state Comptroller or Treasurer to see if the decedent has unclaimed property in that state.

EAGLE PUBLISHING COMPANY OF BOCA lists telephone numbers for the unclaimed property division for each state at their Web site. http://www.eaglepublishing.com

CLAIMS FOR DECEDENT VICTIMS OF HOLOCAUST

The New York State Banking Department has a special Claims Processing Office for Holocaust survivors or their heirs. The office processes claims for Swiss bank accounts that were dormant since the end of World War II. If the decedent was a victim of the Holocaust, you can get information about money that may be due to the decedent's Estate by calling (800) 695-3318.

CLAIMS FOR INCOME TAX REFUNDS

The IRS reports that each year some 2 million taxpayers fail to claim some 3 billion dollars in refunds. Some employees had taxes withheld from their wages but had too little income to file a tax return and may not be aware that the taxes they paid are refundable. Other employees may not have had any tax withheld, but they might be eligible for the refundable Earned Income Tax Credit. The IRS gives taxpayers five years to claim these funds.

You can determine whether they are holding a check for the decedent by calling the IRS at (800) 829-1040. You can get more information about unclaimed tax refunds by visiting the IRS Web site. http://www.irs.gov/

UNCLAIMED STATE TAX REFUNDS

You can check whether the decedent is due a refund on his Oklahoma income tax return by calling the Taxpayer Assistance Division at (800) 522-8165 Extension 13160 or writing to: Oklahoma Tax Commissioner
Taxpayer Assistance
P.O. Box 53249
Oklahoma City, OK 73152-3248

THE LOST PENSION

The decedent may be entitled to benefits under a pension plan of a prior employer. If the decedent worked for an employer for any significant period of time, say 5 years or more, then you need to check with the company benefit representative to determine whether any pension funds are payable. If you are unable to locate the former employer, then it could be that the company moved or merged with another company. There are several ways to track down the company, starting with the Secretary of State to learn of the company's current status (see page 48).

CONTACT THE UNION If company workers belonged to a union, you can contact the union and they may be able to help you locate the company; or tell you what happened to the pension funds.

CONTACT SOCIAL SECURITY The Social Security Administration has the decedent's work record and the employer identification number for each of his employers. The Personal Representative should be able to get that information by calling the Social Security Administration at (800) 772-1213. Using the employer identification number you might be able to determine whether the pension fund was taken over by another company.

RESEARCH THE INTERNET Pension Benefit Guaranty Corporation operates an on-line search tool for those employees whose pension plans were taken over by regulators because the company filed for bankruptcy, or because the company dissolved the plan. All you need do is go to the pension search prompt at their Web site.

PENSION BENEFIT GUARANTY CORPORATION
http://www.pbgc.gov

LOCATE CONTRACTS

If the decedent belonged to a health club or gym, he may have prepaid for the year. Look for the club contract. It will give the terms of the agreement. If you cannot locate the contract, contact the company for a copy of the agreement. If the contract was prepaid, determine whether the agreement provides for a refund for the unused portion. Even if the contract does not provide for a refund, you may be able to get the owner of the gym to agree to assigning the remaining membership to an heir of the decedent's Estate. Such an assignment is good public relations as well as a means of generating new business should the heir decide to purchase his own membership.

SERVICE CONTRACT

Many people purchase appliance service contracts to have their appliances serviced in the event that an appliance should need repair. If the decedent had a security system, he may have had a service contract with a company to monitor the system and contact the police in the event of a break-in.

If the decedent had a service contract, you need to locate it and determine whether it can be assigned to the new owner of the property. If the contract is assignable, the new owner can reimburse the decedent's Estate for the unused portion. If the contract cannot be assigned, then once the property is transferred, try to obtain a refund for the unused portion of the contract.

FILING THE WILL

Anyone who has possession of the decedent's original Will should deposit it with the Probate Court in the county of the decedent's residence. If the decedent owned property in Oklahoma, but did not live here, then the Will needs to be deposited with the Probate Court in the county where the decedent's property is located. Anyone who has the original Will and who fails to or refuses to deposit the Will within 30 days of being notified of the death, can be sued for any loss suffered because of that failure or refusal (OS 58-21).

The judge of the Probate Court will accept an original Will only and not a copy, so it is important to hand carry the original document to the Court. If you are the Personal Representative of the Will, you can give it to your attorney to file with the court as part of the Probate procedure. Make a copy of the Will for your own records before delivering it to the Court or to your attorney.

Special Situation

WILL DRAFTED IN ANOTHER STATE OR COUNTRY

A Will that was drafted in another state or country can be accepted into Probate in Oklahoma, provided:

- ☑ the Will was prepared and signed in accordance with Oklahoma law - or -
- ☑ the Will was prepared and signed according to the laws of the state where it was drafted - or -
- ☑ the Will was prepared and signed according to the laws of the state of the decedent's residence (OS 84-71).

See Chapter 5 for a discussion of what constitutes a valid Will in the state of Oklahoma.

☎ LAWYER

PROBATING THE OUT OF STATE PROPERTY

If the decedent had his residence in Oklahoma and owned property in another state, you may need to conduct the initial Probate in Oklahoma and an *ancillary* (secondary) Probate in the other state. It may need to be the other way around if the decedent lived in another state and owned property in Oklahoma; namely, you may need to conduct the initial Probate in the other state.

If you are going to be Personal Representative, and the decedent owned property in another state or was a resident of another state, before depositing the Will with the Court consult with an experienced Probate attorney <u>in each state</u> to determine where the initial Probate should be conducted. Convenience is important, but there are other things you need to consider:

COST OF PROBATE

Ask each attorney whether the location of the initial Probate procedure will have an effect on the total cost of Probate.

WHO INHERITS THE ESTATE

The Laws of Descent laws vary significantly state to state. If the decedent died without a Will, it is important to determine whether the location of the initial Probate procedure will change the amount each heir will inherit.

ESTATE/INHERITANCE TAXES

Determine whether the location of the initial procedure will have an impact on the amount of taxes that need to be paid.

THE MISSING WILL

People tend to put off making a Will until they think they need to. For many, that need arises when they are elderly and/or seriously ill and have property that they want to leave to someone. It is uncommon for a young person to have a Will; but those who are aged, and with significant assets, usually have one. A survey conducted for the American Association of Retired Persons ("AARP") found that the probability of having a Will increases with age. Forty-four percent of those surveyed who were between the ages of 50 to 54 had a Will. This increased to 85% for those 80 and older. You can find details of the survey at the AARP Web site.

AMERICAN ASSOCIATION OF RETIRED PERSONS
http://research.aarp.org

Those who make a Will usually tell the person they appoint as Executor of the existence of the Will. Chances are, that someone in the decedent's circle of family and friends, knows whether there is a Will. If you believe the decedent had a Will, but you cannot find it, there are at least three places to check out:

⇨ THE CLERK OF THE DISTRICT COURT

Oklahoma law requires that whoever has the original Will must, within 30 days of notice of the death, give it to the person named as Executor of the Will, or deliver it to the District Court in the county of decedent's residence (OS 58-21).

It is a good idea to check with the Clerk in the county where the decedent lived in the chance that someone found the Will and filed it with the Court.

Oklahoma residents can deposit their Will with the judge of the District Court. If the decedent deposited his Will, you should find a receipt for the Will among his belongings (OS 84-81, 84-82). Regardless of whether you find a receipt, you should ask the Clerk of the District Court whether there is any record of the deposit of the Will with the Court.

⇨ THE DECEDENT'S ATTORNEY

Look at the decedent's checkbook for the past few years and see whether he paid any attorney fees. If you are able to locate the decedent's attorney, then call and inquire whether the attorney ever drafted a Will for the decedent, and if so, whether the attorney has the original Will in his possession. If he has the Will, ask him to forward it to the Probate Court in the county of the decedent's residence.

Asking the attorney to forward the Will to the court does not obligate you to employ the attorney should you later find that you need the assistance of an attorney for the Probate administration.

⇨ THE SAFE DEPOSIT BOX

Most people keep their original Will in a safe deposit box. If you believe that the decedent had a Will but you cannot find it, check to see whether the decedent had a safe deposit box. If he did, you will need to gain entry to that box to see whether the Will is in the box.

See page 82 for an explanation of how to gain entry to the safe deposit box.

☎ **LAWYER**

A COPY OF THE WILL AND NO ORIGINAL

A person can revoke his Will simply by destroying it i.e., by ripping it up, burning it or by writing over it in such a manner as to indicate that the Will is cancelled or revoked (OS 84-101). If you have a copy of the Will and cannot find the original, the judge will presume that the decedent revoked his Will by destroying it. If you believe the original was not revoked but is lost, you can ask the Probate Court to admit a copy of the Will to Probate.

Oklahoma courts have allowed a copy of a lost Will to be probated provided the next of kin and all the people who might stand to benefit from the Will, are given notice that the copy is being submitted to the Court for Probate AND it can be proven that:

☑ the document offered is a true copy of the original Will, AND

☑ the decedent did not intend to revoke the Will (OS 58-81).

Not easy things to prove. If you wish to have a lost Will admitted to Probate, you will need to employ an attorney experienced in Probate matters to present your case to the Court.

The surviving spouse, or anyone who leased the safe deposit box jointly with the decedent, may access that box and remove any or all of its contents.

If the decedent was the only person with access to the safe deposit box, then under Oklahoma law the bank (or safe deposit box lessor) may allow any of the following people to examine the contents of the box:

- the decedent's spouse
- a parent of the decedent
- an adult descendant
- the person named as Executor in a copy of the decedent's Will (OS 6-1308(A))

Oklahoma statute requires that an officer of the bank be present when the safe deposit box is opened. If you are any of the above persons and you want to inspect the content of the safe deposit box, call the bank ahead of time and make an appointment to meet with an officer of the company.

If you are gaining access because you are named as the Personal Representative or Executor of the Will, then you need to bring a copy of the Will with you. Ask the bank what other identification they will require of you. Most companies require that you bring a certified copy of the death certificate, so you may need to wait until you receive the death certificate to prove to the bank officials that the owner of the box is dead.

The bank will not allow anything to be removed from the decedent's safe deposit box without a Court order, with the exception of the following

⇨ the original Will, provided the bank keeps a copy

⇨ the decedent's original Trust Agrement, provided the bank keeps a copy

⇨ a deed to the decedent's burial plot

⇨ a life insurance policy, provided it is a policy on the decedent's life and it is given to the beneficiary of the policy (OS 6-1308(A)).

Nothing else may be removed from the safe deposit box until a Personal Representative is appointed and takes possession of the decedent's Probate Estate (OS 6-1308(B)).

The bank is under no duty to take an inventory of the contents of the box, however, they are required to tell the Oklahoma Tax Commissioner that the decedent rented a safe deposit box (OS 6-1308 (D)).

Once you have located the decedent's property you may think the next step is to determine who gets to inherit that property. But some of that property may be needed to pay monies owed by the decedent; so the next step is to determine what, if any, bills need to be paid. And that is the topic of the next chapter.

What Bills Need To Be Paid? 4

The Personal Representative has the duty to be sure that all valid claims against the Estate (demands for payment) are paid. If the decedent had debts, but no money or property, then of course, there is no way to pay the claim. The only remaining question is whether anyone else is responsible to pay for the monies owed. If the decedent was married, the first person the creditor will look to is the decedent's spouse. To understand the basis of this expectation, you need to know a bit of the history of our legal system.

Our laws are derived from the English Common Law. Under early English Common Law, a single woman had the right to own property in her own name and also the right to contract to buy or sell property; but when she married, her legal identity merged with her spouse. She could not hold property free from her husband's claim or control. She could no longer enter into a contract without her husband's permission.

Once married, a woman became financially dependent on her husband. He, in turn, became legally responsible to provide his wife with basic necessities — food, clothing, shelter and medical services. If anyone provided basic necessities to his wife, then regardless of whether the husband agreed to be responsible for the debt, he became obliged to pay for them. This law was called the DOCTRINE OF NECESSARIES.

In the United States, a series of Married Women's Rights Acts were passed giving a married woman the right to own property. The Oklahoma law gives a married woman the same right to contract, own property and run a business in the same manner as any single woman (OS 43-214).

As Married Women's Rights laws were passed state to state, a series of cases tested whether the Doctrine of Necessaries still applied in that state. Questions that judges had to decide were:

> *If a wife can own property and contract to pay for her own necessities, should her husband be responsible for such debts in the event she does not have enough money to pay for them?*
>
> *And if the husband is responsible to pay for his wife's necessities should she be responsible for his?*

In Oklahoma, the legislature answered "yes" to both questions by passing a law (OS 43-209.1) making each of them responsible to pay for the necessities furnished to either of them. Anyone who provides necessities for a married person in this state has the right to demand payment from the spouse — whether or not the spouse agreed to be personally liable to pay for the necessities.

This right continues after death. If a person dies owing money for necessities, his Estate is responsible to pay that debt. If the decedent was married and there is not enough money in his Estate to pay that debt, then in Oklahoma, the creditor has the right to seek payment from the surviving spouse, regardless of whether the spouse agreed to pay the bill.

Whether the creditor can demand money from the surviving spouse for items that are not necessities, depends on whether there they have *joint property*; i.e., property acquired during the marriage. Whether the surviving spouse must use his *separate property* to pay debts is not all that clear. Oklahoma statute (OS 43-208) states that:

(A) Neither husband nor wife, as such, is answerable for the acts of the other.

(B) The separate property of the husband is not liable for the debts of the wife contracted before the marriage.

(C) The separate property of the wife is not liable for the debts of her husband..."

OS 43-208 (A) means that monies owed because of the wrongful act of a spouse, cannot be collected from the separate property of the other spouse. For example, if one spouse is to blame for a car accident, the creditor cannot attempt to collect money from the Separate Property of the other spouse.

OS 43-208 (B) is a puzzler. What about debts run up by the wife after marriage? The statute implies that the husband is responsible to pay for those debts with his separate property, regardless of whether he agreed to be personally liable for that debt. Notice OS 43-208 (C) does not distinguish between debts run up by the husband before or after the marriage. It simply says that the wife is not responsible to pay for her husband's debts with her separate property.

In these days of equal protection under the law, it is questionable, whether this statute would hold up in Court. If a wife's creditor tried to collect monies from the separate property of the husband, the husband could say "If my wife is not responsible to use her separate property to pay my debts, why should I use may separate property to pay for hers?

JOINT DEBTS

A ***joint debt*** is a debt that two or more people are responsible to pay. Usually the contract or promissory note reads that both parties agree to ***joint and several*** liability, meaning they both agree to pay the debt and each of them, individually, agree to be pay the debt. A joint debt can also be in the form of monies owed by one person with payment guaranteed by another person. If the person who owes the money does not pay, then the ***guarantor*** (the person who guaranteed payment) is responsible to pay the debt. Funeral expenses, legal fees to Probate the decedent's Estate are all debts of his Estate. They are not joint debts unless someone guaranteed payment for monies owed.

PAYING FOR THE JOINT DEBT

If another person is jointly responsible for monies owed by the decedent, then that bill should be paid from any joint account held with the decedent. If the joint debtor did not have a joint account with the decedent, then the joint debtor must pay the bill from his/her own funds.

JOINT SPOUSAL RESPONSIBILITY

Hospital and nursing home bills are necessities, so if the decedent was married and there is not enough money in his Estate to pay for these bills, his spouse is responsible for payment, regardless of whether the spouse agreed to be liable for the debt. The surviving spouse is also responsible to pay for joint debts. For example, if they both were authorized to use a credit card, and there is no money in the decedent's Estate, then the spouse must pay the debt. Property taxes are a joint debt if the property was owned by the decedent and his spouse.

JOINT PROPERTY BUT NO JOINT DEBT

Suppose all of the decedent's funds are held jointly with a family member and the joint owner of the bank account did not agree to pay those debts? Can the creditor require that half of the joint funds be set aside to pay the debt? The answer to this question depends on how the account is titled. If the account is held as Tenants In Common, then there are no rights of survivorship. Upon your death, your son will continues to own his share of the account. Your share of the account becomes part of your Probate Estate, and as such is available to pay your debts.

Things are different if the account is a Joint Tenancy with right of survivor. Oklahoma Courts have ruled when a joint tenancy is created, each person owns all of the property. The death of one Joint Tenant does not pass anything to the surviving owner because the survivor already owns all of the property. In such case, your son will own the account with no responsibility to pay your credit card debt (*Clovis v. Clovis*, 460 P.2d 878 (Okla.1969)).

EXCEPTION TO THE RULE

Oklahoma Courts have ruled that if it can be proven that the joint account was established for convenience only, and that the decedent did not intend that the surviving joint owner keep the account funds, the Court can find that the surviving joint owner is holding the account funds in trust for the deceased joint owner. A Trust created in this manner is referred to as a *Resulting Trust*. Once the Court finds that a Resulting Trust exists, all of the monies in the account belong to the Estate of the decedent and as such are available to pay any valid claim (*Branham v. Smith*, 852 P.2d 761 (Okla. 1992)).

NO MONEY — NO PROPERTY

If the decedent owed money then the debt needs to be paid from assets owned by the decedent — which leads to the next question "Did the decedent have any money in his own name when he died?"

If the decedent died without any money or property in his name, then there is no money to pay any creditor. The only question that remains is whether anyone else is liable to pay those bills. The issue of payment most often arises in relation to services provided by nursing homes. When a person enters a nursing home, he is usually too ill to speak for himself or even sign his name. In such cases, the nursing home administrator will ask the spouse or a family member to sign a battery of papers on behalf of the patient before allowing the patient to enter the facility. Buried in that battery of papers may be a statement that the family member agrees to be responsible for payment to the nursing home. If the family member refuses to guarantee payment and the patient's finances are limited, then the facility may refuse to admit the patient.

Under the federal Nursing Home Reform Law, a nursing home that accepts Medicare or Medicaid payments is prohibited from requiring a family member to guarantee payment as a condition of allowing the patient to enter that facility (USC Title 42 §1395i-3(c)(5)(A)(ii)). Nonetheless, it is common practice for a nursing home, in effect, to say "Either someone agrees to pay for the patient's bill or you need to find a different facility."

For those patients who are single, their position is understandable. The nursing home can require payments from the patient's spouse, but if he is single, no one is responsible to make payments should the patient's monies run out. Most nursing homes are business establishments and not charitable organizations. Even not-for-profit organizations must cover their costs. The nursing home must be paid for the services they provide or they soon will be out of business. For an insolvent patient, the solution is to have the patient admitted to the facility as a Medicaid patient.

But suppose the decedent had some money when he entered the nursing home and you agreed to guarantee payment to the nursing home. What if you feel that you were coerced into signing as a guarantor?

Are you now liable to pay the decedent's final nursing home bill if your family member died without funds?

An experienced Elder Law attorney will be able to answer these questions after examining the documents that you signed and the conditions under which the patient entered the nursing home.

If the decedent was married and no Probate procedure is necessary, then the surviving spouse needs to make provision for paying bills they were both responsible to pay. If the decedent was not married and he owned property belonging to him alone, such as a bank account, securities or real property, then paying monies owed by the decedent falls to the Personal Representative.

Once he is appointed, the Personal Representative needs to make a diligent effort to locate all of the decedent's creditors and notify them that they have two months from the date of the notice to file a claim against the decedent's Estate (OS 58-331).

The Personal Representative needs to look over each claim and decide whether that claim is valid. The problem with making that decision is that the decedent is not here to say whether he actually received the goods and services that are now being billed to his Estate.

That is especially the case for medical or nursing care bills. An example of improper billing brought to the attention of this author was that of a bill submitted for a physical examination of the decedent. The bill listed the date of the examination as July 10th, but the decedent died on July 9th. Other incorrect billings may not be as obvious, so each invoice needs to be carefully examined.

If the Personal Representative decides to challenge a bill, and is unable to settle the matter with the creditor, then the Probate Court will decide whether the debt is valid and should be paid.

MEDICAL BILLS COVERED BY INSURANCE

If the decedent had health insurance you may receive an invoice stamped "THIS IS NOT A BILL." This means the health care provider has submitted the bill to the decedent's health insurance company and expects to be paid by them. If the decedent was receiving Medicare, you will receive a ***Medicare Summary Notice*** listing all of the services or supplies that were billed to Medicare for the prior 30 days. In some areas of the country, you can get a copy of the decedent's Medicare Summary Notice from the Internet. To see if it is available in your area, look up e-MSN in the "Frequently Asked Questions" section of the Medicare Web site http://www.medicare.gov.

Even though payment is not requested, it is important to verify that the bill is valid for two reasons:

➢ LATER LIABILITY

If the insurer refuses to pay the claim, the facility will seek payment from whoever is in possession of the decedent's property, and that may reduce the amount inherited by the beneficiaries.

➢ INCREASED HEALTH CARE COSTS

Regardless of whether the decedent was covered by a private health care insurer or Medicare, improper billing increases the cost of health insurance to all of us. Consumers pay high premiums for health coverage. We, as taxpayers, all share the cost of Medicare. If unnecessary or fraudulent billing is not checked, then ultimately, we all pay.

If you believe that you have come across a case of Medicare fraud, you can call the ANTI-FRAUD HOTLINE (800) 447-8477 and report the incident to the Office of the Inspector General of the United States Department of Health and Human Services.

HOW TO CHECK MEDICARE BILLING

The structure of Medicare has been changed giving people in some parts of the country the option of staying with the ***Original Medicare Plan*** or choosing one of the ***Medicare Advantage Plans***. Health care coverage depends on which plan is chosen. If the decedent was covered by Medicare, you need to determine whether he was covered under the Original Medicare Plan, or whether he chose a Medicare Advantage Plan. The publication *Medicare and You* explains coverage under the different options. See page 50 to obtain a copy of the booklet.

Coverage under a Medicare Advantage Plan is explained in the membership materials given to the decedent at the time he signed up for the plan.

BILLING UNDER THE ORIGINAL MEDICARE PLAN

ASSIGNMENT

An important billing question for those under the Original Medicare Plan is whether the health care provider agreed to accept Medicare ***assignment***, meaning that they agreed to accept the Medicare-approved amount. If so, the patient is responsible for the coinsurance rate (usually 20% of the approved amount) and any deductible amount. Doctors and health care providers who do not accept assignment, are limited in the amount they can charge for a Medicare covered service. The highest they can charge is **15%** over the Medicare-approved amount. This ***Limiting Charge*** applies only to certain services and does not apply to supplies and equipment. For more information about assignment you can call (800) 633-4227 for your free copy of *Does your doctor or supplier accept "assignment?"* or you can down-load the publication from the Medicare Web site.

http://www.medicare.gov

ADVANCE BENEFICIARY NOTICE

For those who are in the Original Medicare Plan, a doctor or a supplier may give notice saying that Medicare probably will not pay for the service that is about to be provided. This is called an ***Advance Beneficiary Notice***. If the patient still wants the service after receiving such Notice, he will be asked to sign an agreement stating that he will pay for the service, in the event that Medicare does not pay.

If all of this appears confusing, it is.

To check the decedent's Medicare billing, you need the answers to the following questions:

What is the plan?

Determine whether the decedent was in the Original Medicare Plan or in one of the Medicare Advantage Plans.

What is covered under the plan?

The *Medicare and You* booklet explains what is covered under the Original Medicare Plan. You will need a copy of the membership materials for the Medicare Advantage Plans to determine what is covered under that plan.

Does the Provider accept Assignment?

If the decedent was in the Original Medicare Plan, you need to determine whether the health care provider accepted assignment; and if not whether the Limiting Charge applies to the services provided. If assignment is accepted or the Limiting Charge applies, you need to determine the Medicare-approved amount.

Did the decedent agree to pay?

If the decedent was in the Original Medicare Plan, check to see whether the decedent was given an Advance Beneficiary Notice; and if so, whether he signed a contract agreeing to pay in the event that Medicare refuses to pay.

If the health care provider reports to you that a service provided to the decedent is not covered by Medicare, or if the facility submits the bill and Medicare refuses to pay, check to see if you agree with that ruling by finding answers to the questions on the prior page. You can appeal that decision if you believe that the decedent was wrongly denied coverage.

If the decedent was in the Original Medicare Plan, you will find information about how to file an appeal on the Medicare Summary Notice. If he was part of the Medicare Advantage, you will find that information in his health care plan materials. The book *Your Medicare Rights and Protections* (CMS Pub. No. 10112) contains information about appeals. You can get a free copy by calling (800) 633-4227 or by down-loading it from the Medicare Web site.

www.medicare.gov.

As of July, 2005, the U.S. Department of Health and Human Services will be in charge of Medicare Appeals. They will hold hearings with videoconference equipment or by telephone. They will allow the beneficiary to appeal in person before a judge only if "special or extraordinary circumstances exist." Even if an in-person hearing is allowed, judges will be available in only four locations Miami, Florida, Cleveland, Ohio, Irvine, California and Arlington, Virginia. Beneficiaries who insist on a face-to-face hearing will lose their right to receive a decision within 90 days, so it may take considerable time before the matter is settled.

GETTING HELP WITH THE APPEAL

You can appeal the decision yourself, but it is best to first call the SENIOR HEALTH INSURANCE COUNSELING PROGRAM and learn how to present your case. You can call them at (405) 521-6628. If you want an attorney to assist with your appeal, call the Oklahoma Bar Association Lawyer Referral Service at (918) 584-5243 for a referral to an attorney who is experienced with Medicare appeals.

Some attorneys work *pro bono* (literally for the public good; i.e. without charge) but most charge to assist in an appeal. Federal statute 42 U.S.C. 406(a)(2)(A) limits the amount an attorney may charge for a successful Medicare appeal to 25% of the amount recovered or $4,000, whichever is the smaller amount.

Special Situation DECEDENT ON MEDICAID

Medicaid is a program that provides medical and long term nursing care for people with low income and limited resources. The program is funded jointly by the federal and state government. Federal law requires the state to recover monies spent for a Medicaid recipient who was 55 or older when he received Medicaid assistance. The state will seek reimbursement from the decedent's Estate for the cost of nursing home care, or for home based care, or for other community based services. The state also has a right to recover for money they spent to care for a mentally ill patient in a state institution (OS 43A-4-201).

There usually is no money to recover because to qualify for Medicaid in Oklahoma, a person may not have more than $2,000 in assets. But sometimes it happens that the person on Medicaid dies and his Estate later receives money perhaps as part of a settlement of a lawsuit. Also it could happen that the decedent's home was in his name only. Owning a home does not disqualify a person from receiving Medicaid, however once he dies the state has the right to file a claim on his Estate. Federal law prohibits any recovery of monies spent, until the surviving spouse, and/or disabled child of the decedent are deceased (42 U.S.C. 1396(p)(b)(2)(A)).

The Personal Representative can call the decedent's case worker for information about where to send the notice of the state's right to file a claim.

SOME THINGS ARE CREDITOR PROOF

Sometimes it happens that the decedent had money or property titled in his name only, but he also had a significant amount of debt. In such cases the beneficiaries may wonder whether they should go through a Probate procedure if there will be little, if anything, left after the creditors are paid. Before making the decision consider that some assets are protected under Oklahoma law.

✧ LIFE INSURANCE PROCEEDS ✧

The beneficiary of an insurance policy on the life of the decedent inherits the proceeds of the policy free from the ***claims*** (demand for payment) of creditors. And that is so, regardless of the value of the life insurance policy (OS 36-3631.1).

✧ BENEFITS FROM A FRATERNAL BENEFIT SOCIETY ✧

Any benefit that is payable by a fraternal benefit society (e.g., AARP, American Legion, Kiwanis, Lighthouse for the Blind, Rotary Club, etc.) is free of the monies owed by the decedent. In fact, benefits paid by a fraternal benefit society are free from the claims of the creditors of the member of the society AND from the creditors of the beneficiary (OS 36-2718.1).

✧ WRONGFUL DEATH AWARD ✧

As discussed in Chapter 1, the Personal Representative has the right to bring a law suit on behalf of the decedent's Estate if his death was caused by the wrongful act of a person or company. Up to $50,000 of the wrongful death award is free of the decedent's debts and liabilities. Anything over that value is available to pay his debts with the exception of monies awarded by the Court to punish the wrong doer (OS 31-1(21)).

THE HOMESTEAD EXEMPTION

Every resident of the state of Oklahoma is entitled to a ***Homestead Exemption*** of $5,000. This means that if a person owns his home (including a mobile home) in his name only or jointly with another, then $5,000 of the value of the homestead is exempt from the claims of his creditors. This does not mean the creditor cannot force the sale of the property. It just means that if the property is sold to pay the homeowner's debts, the first $5,000 of the proceeds of the sale goes to the owner. Once a married person dies, his surviving spouse has the right to continue to live in that home for the rest of his/her life. No one can foreclose against the home, with the exception of monies owed for a mortgage or work and construction used to improve the home, or for taxes owed (OS 31-2(c), 31-6).

EXEMPT PERSONAL PROPERTY

The surviving spouse is entitled to keep the following ***Exempt Property*** free from any creditor claim.

- ➪ all family pictures
- ➪ the family bible and other books used as part of the family library up to $100 in value.
- ➪ lots in any burial ground
- ➪ all household and kitchen furniture
- ➪ all wearing apparel and clothing of the decedent and his family
- ➪ one year's supply of family provisions, including fuel for the year

If there is no surviving spouse, the decedent's minor children will inherit these items in equal shares free from any creditor claim (OS 58-311).

✧ PENSION PLANS ✧

Annuities, pensions, profit sharing or other retirement plans regulated by the federal Employee Retirement Income Security Act of 1974 ("ERISA"), including IRA accounts, Keogh accounts and plans identified by the Internal Revenue Code 403(a & b), 457, are creditor proof, provided that contributions made to such plan, by the pensioner, or on his behalf, were not taxable at the time of the contribution. Specifically, if no income tax was due at the time of the contribution, the monies contributed are free from the claims of the decedent's creditors (OS 31-1(20)).

NO EXEMPTION FOR TAXES

Although income taxes are not paid when money is placed in a retirement plan, they are payable when the monies are withdrawn from the account regardless of whether the monies are withdrawn by the retiree or the person he named as beneficiary of the retirement plan. If your beneficiary inherits money from your pension, retirement allowance, or annuity, he may need to pay taxes on those monies.

✧ THERE IS A PRIORITY OF PAYMENT ✧

Next, consider that not all Probate debts are equal. If there are insufficient funds in the Probate Estate to pay for all claims against the decedent's Estate, then Oklahoma Statute 58-591 establishes an order of priority for payment:

CLASS 1: REASONABLE FUNERAL EXPENSES

The reasonable expenses of the decedent's funeral and burial are first in priority (OS 58-591(1)).

CLASS 2: MEDICAL EXPENSES

Second in line is payment for the reasonable and necessary medical expenses of the decedent's last illness, including payment to those who provided nursing or custodial care (OS 58-591(2)).

CLASS 3: FAMILY ALLOWANCE

If the amount set aside as Exempt Personal Property is not enough to support the surviving spouse and children during the Probate proceedings, then once the funeral and medical expenses are paid, the Probate Court can award them a ***Family Allowance.*** The amount awarded by the Court is as much as is reasonably necessary for the maintenance of the family (OS 58-314).

CLASS 4: FEDERAL AND STATE TAXES

Monies or taxes owed by the decedent to the federal or state, county or city government are fourth in line for payment (OS 58-591(4)).

CLASS 5: DEBTS HAVING PREFERENCE

Debts having preference under the laws of Oklahoma or the United States have a Class 5 priority (OS 58-591(5)).

CLASS 6: JUDGMENTS AND LIENS

Judgments against the decedent during his lifetime which are liens against his property are sixth in line for payment. Mortgages also have a Class 6 priority. Judgments and liens have priority in the order of their date (OS 58-591(6)).

CLASS 7: CLAIMS FILED WITHIN TWO MONTHS

The Personal Representative will publish a Notice to Creditors. Any creditor who files a claim within two months of that notice has Class 7 priority (OS 58-591(7)).

CLASS 8: ALL OTHER CLAIMS

All other claims with the exception of a Class 9 claim (OS 58-591(8)).

CLASS 9: INTEREST ON FEDERAL ESTATE OR GIFT TAX

Interest charged because of an extension of time for payment of the federal Estate or Gift Tax is a cost of administration (OS 58-591(9)).

With the exception of a Class 6 priority, there are no priorities within a given class. For example, suppose the decedent left enough money to pay for the his funeral with $20,000 left over. If there are no other debts, his beneficiaries will inherit the $20,000.

Suppose instead that he left a hospital bill of $30,000 and a doctor's bill of $10,000 (both Class 2 debts). The $20,000 will be prorated with the hospital getting $15,000 and the doctor getting $5,000. There will be nothing left to pay any other claim. There will be nothing left for anyone to inherit.

✧ THERE IS A STATUTE OF LIMITATIONS ✧

There are federal and state laws that set time periods for pursuing a claim. Anyone who wishes to take Court action must do so within the time set by the given Statute of Limitation. For example, a law suit for the wrongful death of the decedent must be filed within two years of the death (OS 12-1053(A)).

There is a Statute of Limitations for a creditor to come forward and make a ***claim*** (a demand for payment) against the decedent's Estate. Within two months of receiving his Letters, the Personal Representative is required to publish notice of the death in a newspaper of general circulation once a week for two consecutive weeks. He will also mail notice to any of the decedent's known creditors.

The Notice To Creditors will give the *Presentment Date*, i.e., the date on which all claims must be filed. That date must be at least two months following the date the Notice To Creditors is filed with the Court (OS 58-331).

Claims that are not filed by the Presentment Date are forever barred, but there are exceptions to the rule. The judge can allow the claim at any time prior to the final order distributing the Estate. For example, if decedent owed money on a contract that he signed prior to his death, and the creditor was out of town at the time of the death, and the Personal Representative neglected to give him written notice, the Court can allow the claim even if the Presentment Date has passed (OS 58-333, 58-340).

☎ LAWYER

DECEDENT LEAVING CONSIDERABLE DEBT

If the decedent died leaving much debt and no property, the solution is simple. No Probate — no one gets paid. But if the decedent had property and died owing a significant amount of money the heirs may be tempted to postpone Probate until its too late for a creditor to pursue a particular claim because of the Statute of Limitations.

This may not be the best decision. Some creditors are tenacious and will use whatever legal strategy is available in order to be paid, including initiating the Probate procedure themselves. If the person named of Executor of the decedent's Will does not ask to be appointed as Personal Representative, after 30 days from the date of death, a creditor can petition the Court to be appointed as Personal Representative of the Estate (OS 58-108).

As we will see in Chapter 6, a Personal Representative has much authority when conducting the Probate procedure. Family members may object to having a creditor as a Personal Representative, so there could be a Court battle over who has priority to be appointed as Personal Representative. Court battles are expensive, emotionally as well as financially. Before you decide to distance yourself from the Probate procedure, consult with an attorney experienced in Probate matters for an opinion about the best way to administer the Estate.

MONIES OWED TO THE DECEDENT

Suppose you owed money to the decedent. Do you need to pay that debt now that he is dead? That depends on whether there is some written document that says the debt is forgiven once the decedent dies. For example, suppose the decedent loaned you money to buy your home. If he left a Will saying that once he dies, your debt is forgiven, then you do not need to make any more payments. If you signed a promissory note and mortgage at the time you borrowed the money from the decedent, the Personal Representative should sign the original promissory note **PAID IN FULL** and return the note to you. If the mortgage was recorded, the Personal Representative needs to have a Satisfaction of Mortgage recorded in the county where the property is located. You should receive the recorded Satisfaction for your records.

If you owed the decedent money and there is no Will, or if there is a Will, and no mention of forgiving the debt, then you still owe the money. Monies borrowed from the decedent and his spouse need to be repaid to the spouse. Monies borrowed from the decedent only, become an asset to the Estate of the decedent, meaning that you owe the money to the decedent's Estate. If you are one of the beneficiaries of the Estate, you can deduct the money from your inheritance.

For example, suppose your father left $70,000 in a bank account to be divided equally between you and your brother. If you owed your father $20,000, your father's Estate is really worth $90,000 with each child entitled to $45,000. Instead of paying the $20,000, you can agree to receive $25,000 and have the $20,000 debt forgiven. Your brother will receive the remaining $45,000.

Who Are The Beneficiaries? 5

A question that comes up early on is who is entitled to the property of the decedent. To answer the question you first need to know how the property was *titled* (owned) as of the date of death.

There are three ways to own property. The decedent could have owned property jointly with another person; or in trust for another person; or he could have owned property that was titled in his name only.

In general, upon the decedent's death:

Joint Property with right of survivor belongs to the surviving joint owner.

Trust Property belongs to the beneficiaries of the Trust.

Property owned by the **decedent only** is inherited by the beneficiaries named in the Will. If there is no Will, the property goes to his heirs according to Oklahoma's Laws of Descent.

NOTE ⇨ If the decedent was married, his spouse may have rights in his property.

This chapter describes each type of ownership in detail.

PROPERTY OWNED JOINTLY

Bank accounts, securities, motor vehicles, real property can all be owned jointly by two or more people. If one of the joint owners dies, then the survivor(s) continue to own their share of the property. Who owns the share belonging to the decedent depends on how the joint ownership was set up.

THE JOINT BANK ACCOUNT

When a bank account is opened the depositors sign an agreement with the bank that states the terms and conditions of the account. If the account is opened in two or more names, the contract will say whether each depositor has authority to make a withdrawal, or whether two signatures are necessary. The statement will also say whether there are ***rights of survivorship***. If either party can make a withdrawal from the account, it is presumed that there are rights of survivorship (OS 18-381.39a).

Once an owner of a joint account dies, the surviving owner is free to withdraw all of the monies from the account without the need to go through Probate to get the money; but understanding that he may be responsible to pay Estate Taxes on monies he inherits from the account.

If a survivorship account is held in three names and one owner dies, the share owned by the decedent is divided equally between the surviving owners. Of course, either of the survivors can go to the bank and withdraw all of the funds in the account. With such an arrangement, the surviving owners need to cooperate with each other to divide the funds in the account equitably.

JOINTLY HELD SECURITIES

You can determine whether the decedent owns a security alone or jointly with another by examining the face of the stock or bond certificate. If two names are printed on the certificate followed by a statement that the owners are "joint tenants with rights of survivorship ("JTWRS")," the surviving owner can either cash in the security or ask the company to issue a new certificate in the name of the surviving owner.

Each state has its own securities regulations. If a security held in two or more names, was registered or purchased in another state, and it does not indicate whether there are rights of survivor, you need to contact the company to determine how the account was set up; i.e. with or without rights of survivorship.

If the decedent held his securities in a brokerage account, then the name of the owner of that account is printed on the monthly or quarterly brokerage statement. Not all brokerage firms print the name of a joint owner on the brokerage statement, so you need to contact the firm to determine whether there is a surviving joint owner, or perhaps a beneficiary of the account. Request a copy of the contract that is the basis of the account. The contract will show when the account was opened and the terms of the brokerage account.

JOINTLY OWNED MOTOR VEHICLE

If a motor vehicle is held jointly, the name of each owner is printed on the title to the motor vehicle. Joint ownership is indicated by the words "AND" or "OR." For example, the title can read: HENRY LEE OR DAVID LEE or the title can read: HENRY LEE AND DAVID LEE.

In Oklahoma, it is assumed that there are rights of survivorship when a car is owned jointly. Should one party die, the other can have title changed to his name only by presenting a certified copy of the death certificate to the Motor Vehicle Division of the Oklahoma Tax Commission. They are located at 409 N.E. 28th Street in Oklahoma City, however they have a statewide network of over 300 motor license agents, called ***Tag Agents.***

MOTOR VEHICLE IN DECEDENT'S NAME ONLY

If the decedent's car was in his name only and he left a Will, then the car goes to the beneficiaries named in the Will. If the decedent died without a Will, the car goes to the next of kin as defined the Oklahoma Laws of Descent and Distribution.

Chapter 6 for an explanation of how to transfer title to the motor vehicle.

The name of the owner of real property is printed on the face of the deed. To determine whether the decedent owned the property jointly with another person, you need to look at the last recorded deed. The deed will indicate joint ownership. For example:

KNOW ALL MEN BY THESE PRESENTS:
That ANN TRAYNOR, party of the first part,
in consideration of the sum of $100,000, in hand paid,
the receipt of which is hereby acknowledged,
does hereby grant, bargain, sell and convey unto
ALFRED CODY and SCOTT CODY as
JOINT TENANTS WITH RIGHT OF SURVIVOR,
party of the second part, the following described
real property and premises . . .

Ann Traynor is the ***Grantor*** of the deed. That means she transferred the property to Alfred Cody and Scott Cody who are the ***Grantees*** and present owners of the property. The deed states that Alfred and Scott are JOINT TENANTS WITH RIGHT OF SURVIVOR. Should one of the Grantees die, the surviving joint tenant will own the property 100%. Nothing need be done to establish the ownership, however the decedent's name remains on the deed.

If you are the surviving joint owner of real property you will need to file a Certificate with the Probate Court verifying that no taxes are due on the inheritance. See chapter 6 for information about transferring title to real property (OS 58-912(c)).

DEED HELD AS TENANT IN COMMON

If a deed identifies the decedent and another as TENANTS IN COMMON, then the decedent's share belongs to whomever the decedent named as his beneficiary in his Will. If the decedent died without a Will, Oklahoma's Laws of Descent determine who inherits the decedent's share of the property. A Probate procedure will be necessary to transfer the decedent's share of the property to the proper beneficiary.

There is no implied right of survivorshop. Oklahoma Courts have ruled that a deed that names two or more people as Grantees is a TENANCY IN COMMON ". . . unless it is clearly shown upon the face of the instrument that a joint tenancy with right of survivorship was intended" (*Swanson v. Swanson*, 250 P.2d 40, 207 Okla. 423 (1951)).

DEED HELD AS HUSBAND AND WIFE

If a married couple hold property as follows:

TODD AMES AND SUSAN AMES, TENANTS BY THE ENTIRETY

when one spouse dies, and providing they are married at the time of death, the surviving spouse owns the property 100%. If the deed does not say Tenancy By the Entirety or does not say that they hold the property as Joint Tenants With Rights Of Survivorship, then they hold title as Tenants In Common (OS 60-74).

DEED WITH A LIFE ESTATE

A ***Life Estate*** interest in real property means that the person who owns the Life Estate has the right to live in that property until he/she dies. You can identify a Life Estate interest by examining the face of the deed. If somewhere you see the phrase RESERVING A LIFE ESTATE to the deceased Grantor, the Grantee now owns the property. For example, suppose the granting paragraph of the deed reads:

> Know all men by these presents: that
> ROSE SMITH, a single woman, party of the first part,
> in consideration of the sum of $10 and other good
> and valuable consideration . . . in hand paid,
> the receipt of which is hereby acknowledged,
> does hereby grant, bargain, sell and convey unto
> SAM SMITH, party of the second part,
> RESERVING A LIFE ESTATE TO ROSE SMITH
> . . .

Rose (the Grantor) is the owner of the Life Estate. Sam (the Grantee) is the owner of the ***Remainder Interest***. Rose has the right to occupy the premises during her lifetime or to rent it out and receive the income from the property. During Rose's lifetime, Sam has no right to the possession of, or the income from, the property. Once Rose dies, Sam will own the property and is free to take possession of the property and to lease, sell or transfer it, as he sees fit. No Probate procedure is necessary for him to take possession, however, he may want to have documents recorded so that people will know that he is now the owner. See Chapter 6 for a discussion of transferring real property in Oklahoma.

SPOUSE AN INVISIBLE LIFE ESTATE

As soon as a homeowner in the state of Oklahoma says "I do," his spouse becomes the owner of a Life Estate interest in his home. For example, suppose a single man owns his home and it is titled in his name only. Should he marry, his wife will have the right to live in her husband's home in the event that he dies while owning that home. If they have children, the children have the right to occupy the home until the youngest child reaches the age of 18.

Once the youngest reaches 18, and the wife either dies or voluntarily gives up her right to occupy the homestead, the house will go to the beneficiary of the home as identified in her husband's Will. If he dies without a Will, the property will go to his heirs as determined by Oklahoma's Laws of Descent.

The law applies equally to woman; i.e., if a woman owns her home in her name only, should she die, her husband and minor children have the right to continue to occupy the home until the children are grown and the husband dies

Oklahoma Courts have ruled that the surviving spouse is responsible to pay taxes and any necessary repairs during his/her occupancy of the homestead (*Wells v. Sweeney*, 94 N.W. 394 (1903)). The surviving spouse has the right to continue to occupy the homestead, even though he/she subsequently remarries (*Karbs. v Bouse*, 154 P.2d 968 (1945)).

LAWYER OUT OF STATE PROPERTY

The laws of the state or country where the property is located determine who inherits property in that state. Even if the decedent lived in Oklahoma, property he owned in another state or country is distributed according to the laws of that state or country.

The laws of each state are similar, but not the same. Laws differ in how the deed needs to be worded in order to have a right of survivorship. Some states, like Oklahoma, require the deed to specifically say that there is such right. In such states, a deed held as Joint Tenant without a statement that there are rights of survivorship, is a Tenancy In Common. Other states a do not require the deed to specifically state that there are survivorship rights. In such states a deed held as Joint Tenants means that there are rights of survivorship, even if the deed does not specifically say so. If the decedent owned property in another state, it is important to consult with an attorney in that state to determine who now owns the property.

CAUTION THERE COULD BE A LATER DEED

The above discussion on the different types of ownership of real property assumes that you are in possession the most recent, valid deed. The decedent could have signed another, later deed. Before you come to a conclusion about who inherits the property it is advisable to have a title search by an attorney or a title insurance company to determine the owner of the property as of the decedent's date of death.

BANK/ SECURITY ACCOUNTS

If a bank account or security account is registered in the name of the decedent held "In Trust For" someone, then once the bank has a certified copy of the death certificate, the bank will turn over the account to the beneficiary. If the beneficiary is a minor, and the account balance is under $10,000, the company may give the money to an adult member of the child's family (OS 58-1208(c)). But if the account is over $10,000 the company will not transfer the funds without permission from the Court. Some companies will seek Court approval even if the sum is less than $10,000. If the amount inherited is significant, the Court may decide to appoint a Guardian to manage and protect the property until the child reaches the age of 18.

BANK ACCOUNT HELD BY A TRUSTEE

If the bank or security account is registered in the name of the decedent "as Trustee under a Trust Agreement," that means the decedent was the Trustee of a Trust and the bank will turn over that account to the Successor Trustee of the Trust. Banks usually require a copy of the Trust Agreement or a Certificate that identifies the Successor Trustee, so the bank should be aware of the identity of the Successor Trustee.

MOTOR VEHICLE

If the motor vehicle is held in the name of the decedent "as Trustee," then the motor vehicle continues to be Trust property. The Successor Trustee will need to contact the motor vehicle bureau to have title changed to that of the Successor Trustee. The Successor Trustee will then dispose of the car according to the terms of the Trust Agreement.

REAL PROPERTY

If the decedent had a Trust and put real property that he owned into the Trust, the deed may read something like this:

. . .

JOHN ZAMORA and MARIA ZAMORA, his wife,
party of the first part for consideration paid,
do hereby grant, bargain, sell and convey unto
JOHN ZAMORA, **Trustee of the**
JOHN ZAMORA REVOCABLE TRUST AGREEMENT
DATED FEBRUARY 2, 2004
the following described real property

. . .

The death of the Trustee of a Trust does not change the ownership of the property. It remains in the Trust. The Trust document might say whether the person who takes John's place as Trustee (the Successor Trustee) should sell or keep the property or perhaps give it to a beneficiary.

If no instruction is given, the Successor Trustee can use his discretion as to what to do with the property. If you are a beneficiary of the Trust and are concerned about what the Successor Trustee will do with the property, then it is best to consult with your attorney to learn about your rights under that Trust.

If the decedent owned property that was in his name only (not jointly or in trust for someone), then some sort of Probate procedure will be necessary before the heirs can get possession of that property. Who is entitled to the decedent's Probate Estate depends on whether the decedent died with or without a Will. If the decedent died ***testate*** (with a Will), then the beneficiaries of the decedent's property are identified in the Will.

If the decedent died without a Will, then Oklahoma's Laws of Descent determine who inherits the decedent's Probate Estate and what percentage of the Probate Estate each heir is to receive once all the bills and costs of administering the Probate procedure are paid.

The law recognizes the right of the family to inherit the decedent's property. The law covers all possible relationships beginning with the decedent's spouse.

Who Is The Spouse?

In this era of people challenging the concept of the family unit, those of a philosophical bent may ponder the meaning of marriage. Is it a union of two people in the eyes of God? Is it even a union? The state of Oklahoma does not concern itself with such things. If a person dies without a Will, then the state will distribute the decedent's Probate Estate according to the laws of the state; and the laws of the state of Oklahoma determine whether two people are married.

BEING MARRIED IN OKLAHOMA

Oklahoma statute (OS 43-1) defines marriage as a personal relationship arising out of a civil contract that is entered into according to Oklahoma law. Specifically, the man and woman must obtain a license to marry from a judge or Clerk of the District Court and then solemnize the marriage by a state or religious ceremony. Parental consent to marry is required for anyone under 18. Court permission is required if either party is under 16 (OS 43-3(B)).

Oklahoma law specifically prohibits the marriage of people who are:

- ☒ ***ancestors*** (parent, grandparents, etc.) or ***descendants*** (child, grandchild, etc.);
- ☒ stepfather and stepdaughter
- ☒ stepmother and stepson
- ☒ aunt and nephew or uncle and niece, except where the relationship is only through marriage, such as a brother-in-law marrying the niece of his ex-wife.
- ☒ brother and sister. This includes siblings who are half blood; i.e. they have only one parent in common.

Oklahoma law bars marriages between first cousins; however if the couple were married in a state that allows first cousins to marry, then that marriage is recognized as being valid in the State of Oklahoma (OS 43-2).

☒ BIGAMY

It is against the law for a married person to marry. No license can be granted if one of the parties is currently married (OS 21-881).

THE COMMON LAW MARRIAGE

A Common Law marriage is one that has not been solemnized by ceremony. It is more than just living together. The couple agree to live together as man and wife, and then publicly hold themselves out as being married; i.e., tell friends, family and business acquaintances that they are married. Oklahoma Courts generally recognize a Common Law marriage as being valid, provided there are no legal impediments to the union. For example, someone who is currently married, cannot enter into a Common Law marriage with another person (*Tatum v. Tatum*, 736 P.2d 506, Okla. 1982)).

INDIAN MARRIAGES

Oklahoma Courts recognize marriages that are entered into according to Indian Custom as being valid in the state of Oklahoma. Courts have ruled "Such marriages are not to be treated as common-law marriages, but as legal marriages according to the customs of the tribe." (*Mayse v. Newman*, 118 P.2d 398 (Okla. 1941)).

SAME SEX MARRIAGES

Vermont is the first state to recognize a same sex marriage, which they refer to as a "civil union." Several other states including Oklahoma, have passed statutes, specifically denying marital status to couples of the same gender. The state of Oklahoma will not recognize a same sex marriage, even though such marriage may be valid in another state (OS. 43-3.1).

It is important to consult with an attorney if you have any question about the validity of the decedent's marriage.

If the decedent died *intestate* (without a Will), the state of Oklahoma provides one for him in the form of its ***Laws of Descent and Distribution***. These laws are also referred to as the *Laws of Intestate Succession*. Once his debts, funeral expenses, and costs of the Probate are paid, whatever is left (his net Probate Estate) is distributed as follows:

✧ CHILD, NO SPOUSE

The descendants (child, grandchild, great-grandchild, etc.), of a single decedent are entitled to his Net Probate Estate. If he had two or more children, all who survive him, then each child is entitled to an equal share of his Estate. If a child died before his parent and the deceased child left surviving descendents, they inherit the share intended for the deceased child ***by right of representation***. Oklahoma statute (OS 84-213(B)(4)) defines "by right of representation" as follows:

> . . .by right of representation means the estate is to be divided into as many equal shares as there are surviving heirs in the nearest degree of kinship and deceased persons in the same degree who left issue who survive the decedent, each surviving heir in the nearest degree receiving one equal share and the equal share of each deceased person in the same degree being divided among his issue in the same manner.

If you understood the above, and you are not a lawyer, then you missed your calling. For the rest of us (even lawyers) its a head-scratcher. Perhaps the best way to explain "by right of representation" is through example.

Suppose the decedent was unmarried with 4 children, Ann, Barry, Carl, David. If he dies without a Will, and all his children survive him, each inherit 25% of his Estate.

CHILD WITHOUT DESCENDANT DIES BEFORE DECEDENT

If Ann dies before her father leaving no descendants, then Barry, Carl and David divide the Estate between them. Each gets one third.

CHILD WITH DESCENDANT DIES BEFORE DECEDENT

Suppose instead that only Carl and David survived their father. If Ann died leaving two children and Barry died leaving one child, the Estate is divided into 4 shares — one for each surviving child and one share for each deceased child who left a descendant. Carl and David each get their 25% share. Ann's two children share her 25% (they each get 12 1/2%). Barry's child receives the share intended for Barry, namely 25% of the Estate.

✧ MARRIED, WITH DESCENDANTS ✧

The surviving spouse is entitled to half of all of the property acquired by the "joint industry of the husband and wife" during the marriage; i.e., their ***Joint Property***. The decedent's children inherit the other half by right of representation.

Property owned prior to the marriage, or property inherited or received property as a gift, is the decedent's ***Separate Property***. If the decedent was married, and all of his children were those of the surviving spouse, the spouse takes half the Separate Property. The other half goes to the children, by representation. If one or more of the decedent's children are not that of the surviving spouse, the Separate Property is shared equally by the spouse and children. The share intended for a deceased child go to his descendant, by representation (OK 84-213(A)).

✧ MARRIED, NO DESCENDANT ✧

If the decedent was married, with no descendant, but a surviving parent, the spouse inherits all of the couple's joint property, and one-third of the decedent's Separate Property. The parents share the other two-thirds. If only one parent survives, he inherits the two-thirds share. If neither parent survives the decedent, the two-third share is inherited by the decedent's surviving brothers and sisters in equal shares. The surviving spouse inherits the entire Estate if the decedent was not survived by a descendant, parent, or sibling (OS 84-213(B)(1).

✧ SINGLE, NO DESCENDANT ✧

If the decedent was single, with no descendants, his Probate Estate is divided equally between the parents. If only one parent is alive, then all of the Net Probate Estate goes to that parent. If neither parent is alive, the Estate is inherited by the decedent's brothers and sisters in equal shares, by representation. There is no distinction between full blood siblings or half blood siblings. For example, if the decedent had one brother with the same set of parents, and another brother with the same father and a different mother, both brothers inherit an equal amount, with one exception. Property that the decedent inherited, or received by a gift from an ancestor cannot be inherited by a half brother or sister who is not the blood of that ancestor (OS 84-222).

If the decedent had no brothers, sisters, nephews or nieces, the Probate Estate is divided with half going to his paternal grandparents. If neither grandparent survives him, that half goes to their descendant by the right of representation. The other half of the Probate Estate is inherited by his maternal grandparents, in the same manner. If he is survived only by grandparents or descendants on one side of the family, they inherit all of his Estate (OS 84-213(B)(2)).

OKLAHOMA: HEIR OF LAST RESORT

In Oklahoma, property that is either unclaimed or abandoned, goes to the state, so if the decedent died without a Will and absolutely no next of kin, then the state of Oklahoma "inherits" his Probate Estate. The state uses the money to support the school system (OK 84-213(B)(3)).

The explanation in this book of the laws of intestate succession is abridged. Even though you may now know more about Oklahoma's Laws of Descent than you ever wanted to know, there is much more to the law. For example, we did not give specific examples of how the Estate is distributed if the decedent is survived only by descendants of his grandparents. We could give an example explaining the law, but we thought you might enjoy a puzzle instead:

Winston died intestate leaving $100,000. His only relatives are his mother's sister, Aunt Susie, and her children, Ramona and Abigail and a first cousin Elvis, on his father's side. How much does each relative receive?

You can check your answer by visiting the puzzle section of the Eagle Publishing Company Web site:

http://www.eaglepublishing.com

CAUTION IT ISN'T ALL THAT SIMPLE

Those who try the given puzzle will appreciate how complex the Oklahoma Laws of Descent can be. Unless the descent is straight forward, with the decedent leaving a surviving spouse and/or children (all who survive him), it is best to consult with an attorney before you decide who is entitled to inherit the decedent's property.

THE RIGHTS OF A CHILD

THE NON-MARITAL CHILD

A child born out of wedlock has the same rights to inherit from his natural father as does one born in wedlock, provided any one of the following are true:

☑ The decedent signed a declaration in the presence of a competent witness that he is the child's father.

☑ After the child's birth the decedent married the child's mother and acknowledged the child as his own, or adopted the child into his family.

☑ He publicly acknowledged the child as his own and if married, receives the child into his home with the consent of his wife.

☑ There was a paternity proceeding and the Court found him to be the child's father (OS 84-215).

☑ He signed an *Affidavit* (a statement sworn to before a notary public) acknowledging his paternity and the Affidavit is filed with the Office of the State Registrar of Vital Statistics (OS 63-1-311.3).

If the decedent denied he is the child's father, it will take a court procedure to establish (or disprove) paternity.

THE AFTERBORN CHILD

Under Oklahoma law a child conceived prior to death and born to the surviving spouse after the death, has the same right to inherit as any other natural child of the decedent (OS 84-173).

THE ADOPTED CHILD

An adopted person who was a minor at the time of adoption has the same right to inherit property under the Laws of Descent from his adoptive parents as does a natural child. The adopted child has no right to inherit from his natural parents, with the exception of the natural parent who is married to the adoptive parent.

For example, if a child loses a parent and is later adopted by a step-parent, the child has the right to inherit from his natural parents and from his adoptive parent as well (OS 10-7505-6.5(A)).

THE CHILD OF AN ASSISTED CONCEPTION

Medical technology has made important contributions to solving the problem of infertility. There are all sorts of solutions, from hormone replacement therapy, to sperm banks that provide donations anonymously, to frozen sperm and/or ova to be thawed and used at a later date, to women who become a surrogate or gestational mother. Solving a set of medical problems has opened the door to a new set of legal problems. Used to be, the only question was "Who's the father?" Now it could well be "Who's the mother?

To answer these questions, the State of Oklahoma has passed laws to legally establish the parentage of children whose conception was assisted by medical technology. We will examine the law as it relates to the right of the child to inherit property.

CHILD OF ARTIFICIAL INSEMINATION

Under Oklahoma law, any child born to a couple through the use of artificial insemination is considered to be the child of those parents; provided, the husband and wife give their written consent for the procedure. The consent must also be signed by the physician who performs the technique, and the judge who is in charge of adoptions. The original document is filed with the Court under seal; i.e., no one may examine the document except under Court order.

Once the child is born, the husband and wife are listed on the birth certificate as the child's natural parents. The child has all of the rights as any other natural child born of his parents. Under Oklahoma law, the donor of the egg or sperm cell has no right or obligation to the child and vice versa. The child has no right or obligation to the donor (OS 10-551, 10-552, 10-553, 10-554, 10-555).

Still another legal issue raised because of modern technology is the question of the rights of the Surrogate mother as opposed to the rights of the biological parent who contracted with the Surrogate to bear his/her child.

THE SURROGATE PARENTING CONTRACT

A Surrogate Parenting Contract is an agreement, usually between a married couple and a woman, in which the woman agrees to be the birth mother of a child conceived with the sperm of the husband, or the egg cell of the wife, or the embryo of the married couple. This means that the husband or wife is the biological parent of the child born of the Surrogate mother. Some states such as New York and Michigan consider Surrogate Parenting Contracts to be against public policy.

Other states, such as Florida and Virginia allow a couple to contract with a woman to have their baby, provided the parties conform to the law of the state.

The state of Oklahoma does not have a law specifically dealing with a Surrogate Parenting Contract, however, in the year 2000, the Oklahoma legislature passed a statute (OS 10-556) relating to the transplantation of a human embryo. The law is the much the same as statutes 10-551 through 10-555. The donor gives up all parental rights. This being the case, a child born to a Surrogate mother is the child of that mother. If she is married, and her husband agreed to the procedure, then he is the legal father of the child. After birth the Surrogate parents can agree to the adoption of the child by the intended (genetic) parents. Adoption is necessary, regardless of whether either (or both) of the intended parents happen to be the genetic parent of the child. If the child is later adopted, the child will have the same status as any other adopted child.

WHO DIED FIRST?

Sometimes it happens that two family members die simultaneously, and no one knows who died first. For example, suppose a husband and wife die together in a car crash, how is the property distributed in that case?

Oklahoma statute provides for an orderly distribution of their respective Estates.

JOINTLY OWNED PROPERTY

Property owned jointly by the couple, with no provision for who is to inherit the property should they both die, is divided with half going to the Estate of the husband and the other half to the Estate of the wife. If they each have a Will, the husband's half is distributed according to his Will and the wife's half according to her Will. If they die without a Will, then each half is distributed according to Oklahoma's Laws of Descent (OS 58-1003).

PROCEEDS OF A LIFE INSURANCE POLICY

Suppose the husband is insured, with his wife as the beneficiary of his life insurance policy. The proceeds of the policy will be distributed as if the wife died before her husband. The proceeds will be given to the alternate beneficiary named in the policy. If no alternate beneficiary was named, the proceeds of the policy will go to the insured party (in this case, the husband) (OS 58-1005).

These same laws apply even if the parties are related in some other manner, such as parent and child; i.e., if they die simultaneously, then the property of the parent is distributed as if he survived the child and the child's property is distributed as if he survived the parent (OS 58-1001, 58-1002).

Special Situation

NO SHARE FOR KILLER

Under Oklahoma law anyone found guilty of the murder of the decedent, or who is found guilty of being an accessory to the crime, is prohibited from profiting from the crime. Property that the killer, or accessory, would have inherited as a beneficiary of the decedent's Will will be distributed to the decedent's *heirs*, i.e., whoever is entitled to inherit according to Oklahoma's Laws of Descent.

One the Court finds the killer guilty of murder, property that was owned by the decedent and the killer (or his accomplice), may not inherit as a beneficiary the decedent's a Pay On Death account or a Transfer On Death security. The killer, or accessory may not take any the decedent's share of a joint account. The share intended for the killer or accessory will be distributed according to the Oklahoma Laws of Descent.

Similarly, the killer, or accessory, may not receive the proceeds of a life insurance policy on the decedent's life, provided that before the proceeds are paid, someone notifies the insurance company, in writing, that the decedent's heirs intend to make a claim based on the Oklahoma statute that bars inheritance by a killer or accessory (OS 84-231).

WHEN TO CHALLENGE THE WILL

It is not uncommon for a family member to be unhappy with the way the decedent willed his property. If you are tempted to challenge a Will, first consider whether the Will is valid under Oklahoma law. In Oklahoma, a Will is presumed valid if at the time the decedent made the Will he was at least 18, and of sound mind (OS 84-41(A)).

Oklahoma Courts have ruled that a Will maker is considered to be of sound mind at the time he made the Will:

☑ he knew what he was doing (i.e., making a Will)

— and —

☑ he knew in a general way what property he had

— and —

☑ he understood his relationship to those who ought to be in his thoughts when making his Will

(*Matter of Estate of Samochee*, 542 P.2d 498 (Okla 1975).

☒ THE UNWITNESSED WILL

The first step in the Probate procedure is to have the Probate court determine whether the Will presented is valid. There should be no problem in having the Will accepted into Probate, provided the Will is in writing and signed by the Will maker in the presence of at least two credible witnesses. But suppose the decedent wrote out a Will in his own hand and signed it with no one present? A Will is written in the Will maker's own hand is called a ***holographic Will.***

Many states refuse to accept an unwitnessed holographic Will into Probate. Oklahoma law allows an unwitnessed holographic Will into Probate provided it is written, dated and signed all in the Will maker's own hand (OS 84-54).

But the problem with an unwitnessed holographic Will is its authenticity. Because no one saw the decedent sign the Will, it is hard to determine whether the Will was written by the decedent or is a forgery. If all the decedent left was a holographic Will, you need to consult with an attorney experienced in Probate matters, to present evidence to the court that the Will is valid.

☒ THE WILL WITNESSED BY A BENEFICIARY

Neither of the witnesses of the decedent's Will should be a beneficiary of the Will. Under Oklahoma law a witness is not entitled to a gift under the Will unless there are two other competent witnesses. In the absence of other witnesses, the Will can be considered valid, but the beneficiary is entitled to only as much as he would have received if the decedent died without a Will, i.e., according to the Laws of Descent (OS 84-143, 84-144).

☒ UNDUE INFLUENCE

The problem with having a beneficiary present when the decedent signed the Will is one of ***undue influence***. Undue influence occurs whenever someone exerts such pressure on the Will maker so that he is not acting according to his own free will. Proving undue influence is about as difficult as trying to prove that the Will maker was of unsound mind. Oklahoma courts have ruled that all the facts and circumstance of the case must be examined ". . . the association of the parties, opportunity for undue influence afforded the person who is especially favored by the terms of the will, and the effect of the will upon those persons whom we would naturally expect to be the recipients of his bounty, must all be considered." (*Matter of Estate of Seegers*, 733 P.2d 418 (Okla. 1986)).

☒ THE VERBAL WILL

Picture a death bed scene. The elderly gentleman is surrounded by several family members. In a whisper, just audible enough to be heard, he says: "Even though I am a wealthy man, I never got around to making a Will. You all have been good to me, but I did want my entire fortune to go to my nephew, Robert. He has been like a son to me."

Do you think Robert can inherit his Uncle's Estate?
Not in Oklahoma unless:

- ➪ The uncle or someone, at his direction, writes down the uncles's wishes in the presence of at least two witnesses AND
- ➪ The uncle or someone, at his direction, signs the Will AND
- ➪ The uncle acknowledges and declares that this writing is his Will AND
- ➪ The uncle asks the witnesses to sign the Will as witnesses
- ➪ The witnesses sign at the end of the Will, verifying that they witnessed all of the above (OS 84-55).

Considering that the uncle's relatives will probably inherit the fortune under the Oklahoma's Laws of Descent , it is doubtful that Robert is in danger of becoming wealthy at any time in the near future.

A VERBAL WILL FOR SOLDIERS

Oklahoma law allows a verbal Will provided the decedent expected to die from an injury he received that day, or he was a soldier or sailer in combat. The gift is limited to $1,000 in value, and the decedent must have made his wishes known in the presence of two witnesses, one of whom he asked to bear witness that this was his Will (OS 84-46).

☒ THE WILL THAT IS CONTRARY TO LAW

Sometimes a person who is of sound mind, makes a Will, but that Will has the effect of giving a spouse or a minor child less than is required under Oklahoma law. One such example is that of Nancy. Hers was not an easy life. She worked long hours as a waitress. She divorced her hard drinking first husband. The final judgment gave her their home, some securities, and sole custody of their son. After the divorce Nancy had her attorney prepare a Will leaving all she owned to her son, Richard.

Some years later she met and married Harry, a chef at the restaurant where she worked. He moved into her home and they later had a daughter. Richard was 19, and his half-sister 12, when Nancy died after a lengthy battle with cancer. Nancy did not leave much — her car, her home, and the securities now worth about $50,000, all were in Nancy's name only.

Before she died, she told Richard that she had not changed her Will because she wanted him to have all she owned. She said Harry had a good job and she was sure he would take good care of his daughter.

No sooner was the funeral over, when stepson came in and demanded that Harry vacate his mother's home. Harry was furious and went to his attorney. "Richard is demanding that I get out of the house and give me the keys to Nancy's car. Can he do that to me?"

The attorney reassured him. "No. Under Oklahoma law, you and your daughter have the right to continue to live in the home until the Probate procedure is over. In fact, you have the right to live in the home until you die (OS 58-311).

"Is that all I get? The right to live in my home? I was a good husband to Nancy, supporting and taking care of her all during her illness. It was me, and not her son, who was at her side when she died. Don't I have any other rights?"

The attorney continued "You also have rights provided you did not give up those rights by signing an *Antenuptial* (premarital) A greement. Did you sign any such document before you married?

"Absolutely not!"

"Then you are entitled to half of the property acquired by your joint efforts" (OS 84-44(a)).

"Is that all? The only thing we acquired by our joint efforts was the car that was in Nancy's name. She owned the house and the securities before we married."

"The judge can award a Family Allowance for you and your daughter's maintenance while Probate is being conducted (OS 58-314).

"Is that her only right?"

"No. Under Oklahoma law, your daughter was born after the date of Nancy's Will so your daughter is entitled to inherit as much as she would have inherited had her mother died without a Will, unless it appears from the Will that the omission was intentional (OS 84-131, 84-132).

"No the Will makes no mention of children born after the Will was signed."

"Nancy had children from her first marriage, so Nancy's Separate Property is divided by a sum equal to the number of her children, plus one for the surviving spouse. In other words, three equal shares. Nancy's Separate Property consists of her securities and her house. You daughter is entitled to one-third of the value of those items. Her children are entitled share equally in Nancy's half of her Joint Property. The car was the only item of Joint Property Your daughter is entitled to half of Nancy's half, namely one quarter the value of the car."

Richard did not fare as well as his mother intended. The judge awarded a Family Allowance for the daughter's support while the Estate was being probated. The car and securities had to be sold to pay for the Family Allowance, the funeral and medical bills and the cost of Probate. All that Richard inherited was his mother's home, one-third of which belonged to his half sister. His step-father had the right to live in the home for the rest of his life, so Richard would wait a long time to get his inheritance (OS 58-311).

No doubt Nancy did not understand what would happen to her Estate once she passed on. The Will she left did not accomplish her goal of providing for her son. All it did was cause turmoil and an irreparable rift between Harry and Richard. It didn't need to be that way. Had Nancy known about Oklahoma law, she could have consulted with an attorney and set up an Estate Plan that could have provided for her son without alienating her husband.

But, the moral of the story, for the purpose of this discussion, is that if you believe that the decedent's Will is not valid or is not drafted according to Oklahoma law, then you need to consult with an attorney experienced in Probate matters to determine your legal rights under that Will.

Getting Possession Of The Property 6

Knowing who is entitled to receive the decedent's property is one thing. Getting that property is another. As explained in the previous chapter, if the decedent held property jointly, or in a Trust for, someone the property now belongs to the joint owner or beneficiary. If it is personal property such as a bank account or a security, the beneficiary can usually get possession of the property by giving a certified copy of the death certificate to the financial institution.

If the decedent had real or personal property in his name only, or if he held property as a Tenant In Common, some sort of Probate proceeding may be necessary in order to transfer ownership to the proper beneficiary. The assistance of an attorney may be required should a full Probate proceeding be necessary, but there are many items that can be transferred without legal assistance. This chapter explains how to get possession of those items.

The chapter also contains an explanation of the different kinds of Probate procedures and when it is appropriate to use that procedure.

Too often, the first person to discover the body will help himself to the decedent's ***personal effects*** (clothing, jewelry, appliances, electrical equipment, cameras, books, stamp or coin collection, household items and furnishing, etc.). Unless that person is the decedent's sole beneficiary, such action is unconscionable, if not illegal.

The decedent may have left a writing, separate from his Will, making a gift of his ***tangible personal property*** (clothing, jewelry, etc. but not money gifts or securities). To be distributed as part of a Probate proceeding, the writing needs to be included in the decedent's Will or written, signed and dated in his own hand(0S 84-54). If Probate is not necessary, the item can just be given to the beneficiary as directed in the separate writing.

The decedent's spouse, or if no spouse, his dependent or minor children are entitled to keep the decedent's household furnitur free of his creditor's claims (OS 58-311). See page 101 for a complete list of Exempt items. In all other cases, his personal effects should be given to the person appointed as the Personal Representative to be distributed according to the decedent's Will, or if no Will according to the Oklahoma Laws of Descent.

If no Probate proceeding is necessary, his next of kin, as determined by the Oklahoma Laws of Descent, need to divide the decedent's personal effects among themselves in approximately equal proportions.

What's Equal?

The decedent's Will may direct that the decedent's personal property be divided equally between two or more beneficiaries. The problem with the term "equal" is that people have different ideas of what "equal" means. Unless there is clear evidence that the decedent's Will meant something else, "equal" refers to the monetary value of the item and not to the number of items received. For example, to divide the decedent's personal effects equally, one beneficiary may receive an expensive item of jewelry and another beneficiary may receive several items whose overall value is approximately equal to that single piece of jewelry.

When distributing personal effects there needs to be cooperation and perhaps compromise, or else bitter arguments might arise over items of little monetary value. One such argument occurred when an elderly woman died who was rich only in her love for her five children and ten grandchildren. After the funeral, the children gathered in their mother's apartment. Each child had his own furnishings and no need for anything in the apartment. They agreed to donate all of their mother's personal effects to a local charity with the exception of a few items of sentimental value.

Each child took some small item as a remembrance — a handkerchief, a large platter that their mother used to serve family dinners, a doily their mother crocheted. Things went smoothly until it came to her photograph album. Frank, the youngest sibling, said, "I'll take this." Marie objected saying "But there are pictures in that album that I want."

Frank retorted, "You already took all the pictures Mom had on her dresser."

The argument went downhill from there. Unsettled sibling rivalries boiled over, fueled by the hurt of the loss that they were all experiencing. It almost came to blows when the eldest settled the argument: "Frank you make copies of all of the photos in the album for Marie. Marie, you make copies of all of the pictures that you took and give them to Frank. This way you both will have a complete set of Mom's pictures. And while you're at it, make copies for the rest of us."

NONPROBATE TRANSFERS

A ***Nonprobate transfer*** is a transfer of the decedent's property without the need for Probate. For example, if the decedent had a bank account in his name only "In Trust For" someone or with instructions to "Pay On Death" to someone, all the beneficiary need do is produce a death certificate and proper identification, and the bank will turn over the property to the beneficiary.

Securities that are held jointly with someone, or with instructions to "Transfer On Death" to a named beneficiary, can be transferred to that beneficiary in the same manner. The beneficiary of a Nonprobate transfer needs to keep in mind that he may be required to contribute the Nonprobate asset to pay monies owed by the decedent. But only if there are no other assets to pay the debt.

The Personal Representative must use the Probate Estate to pay monies owed. If there are not sufficient funds, he will look to the Successor Trustee of the decedent's ***Inter Vivos Trust***; i.e. a Trust established by the decedent during his lifetime that contains most of his assets.

If there is no Inter Vivos Trust, or if the funds in the Trust are insufficient to pay the bills, the Personal Representative will look to the beneficiaries of all Nonprobate transfers to contribute a proportionate share to pay such bills.

The Personal Representative will not seek Nonprobate assets unless the surviving spouse, or child or creditor makes a written demand to seek Nonprobate assets to pay bills. That demand must be made within a year of the death (OS 71-910). In general, if no demand is made within that time, the beneficiary is free to keep the gift.

TRANSFERRING A CAR OWNED JOINTLY

As explained in the last chapter, no Probate proceeding is necessary if title to the decedent's car was held jointly with another; i.e., title is held in the decedent's name and another separated by the word "AND" or "OR." The surviving joint owner can go to the nearest Tag Agent and transfer the car to his name only. He can do this on his signature alone, provided there is no lien on the car. If monies are owed on the car, title to the car cannot be changed until the lien is released.

TRANSFERRING THE CAR

If a Probate proceeding is necessary, then regardless of its value, it is the job of the Personal Representative to transfer the car to the proper beneficiary. If the Will makes a *specific gift* of the car, the Personal Representative will transfer the car to that person. If there was no mention of the car in the decedent's Will, it goes to the ***residuary beneficiaries*** under the Will, i.e., those who inherit whatever is left once all the bills have been paid and all the special gifts made in the Will are distributed. If the decedent did not have a Will, then the car goes to the decedent's heirs as determined by Oklahoma's Laws of Descent.

TRANSFER WHEN MORE THAN ONE BENEFICIARY

If there is more than one person who has the right to inherit the car, then they all can take title to the car. That may not be a practical thing to do since only one person can drive the car at any given time and if one gets into an accident, they all can be held liable. The better route is for the beneficiaries to agree to have one person take title to the car. The person taking title will need to compensate the others for their share of the car. In such case the beneficiaries need to come to an agreement as to the value of the car.

DETERMINING THE VALUE OF THE CAR

Cars are valued in different ways. The *collateral* value of the car is the value that banks use to evaluate the car for purposes of making a loan to the owner of the car. If you were to trade in a car for the purpose of purchasing a new one, the car dealer would offer you its *wholesale* value. Were you to purchase that same car from a car dealer, he would price it at its *retail* or *fair market value*. Usually the retail price is highest, wholesale is lowest and its collateral value is somewhere in between.

You can call your local bank to get the collateral value of the car. It may be more difficult to obtain the wholesale value because the amount of money a dealer is willing to pay depends on the value of the new car that you are purchasing. You can determine the car's retail value by looking at comparable used car advertisements in the local newspaper.

Rather than going through the effort of determining these three values, you can use your Internet search engine to look up the Kelly Blue Book Value. This publication gives Low, Average and High Blue Book Values which correspond to the wholesale, collateral and retail values.

Once the fair market value of the car is determined, the beneficiary who takes the car will be considered to have received that value as part of his inheritance. If none of the beneficiaries want the car, the Personal Representative will sell it and add the proceeds to the amount distributed to the beneficiaries.

It is a good idea to limit the use of the car until it is sold or transferred to the beneficiary. If the decedent's car is involved in an accident before the car is transferred to the new owner, the decedent's Estate may be liable for the damage. Having adequate insurance on the car may save the Estate from monetary loss, but a pending lawsuit could delay Probate and prevent any money from being distributed to the beneficiaries until the lawsuit is settled.

MAKING THE TRANSFER

You can get title and registration information at the Oklahoma Tax Commission Web site.

OKLAHOMA TAX COMMISSION
http://www.oktax.state.ok.us/

Special Situation

TRANSFERRING THE LEASED CAR

The leased car is not an asset of the Estate because the decedent did not own the car. The decedent was obligated to pay the balance of the monies owed on the lease agreement, so the car is a liability to the Estate. The Personal Representative needs to work out an agreement with the company to either assign the lease to someone who agrees to pay the balance of the lease — or have the Estate pay off the lease by purchasing the car under the terms of the lease agreement.

Some lenders will allow the lease to be assigned provided the Estate remains liable for the balance of payment. In such cases, it is better to have the car refinanced and have the original lease paid in full.

If the remaining payments exceed the current market value of the car, there may be a temptation to hand the keys over to the leasing company. This may not be the best strategy, because the leasing company can sell the car and then sue the Estate for the balance of the monies owed. If the decedent had no assets or if the only assets he had are creditor proof, simply returning the car may be an option. But if the decedent's Estate has assets available to pay the balance of the lease payments, the Personal Representative needs to arrange to have the car transferred in a way that releases the Estate from all further liability.

TRANSFERRING THE MOBILE HOME

Before transferring the motor vehicle, you need to find out whether the land on which the mobile home is located was leased or owned by the decedent. If the decedent was renting space in a trailer park, you need to contact the trailer park owner to transfer the lease agreement to the beneficiary of the mobile home. If the decedent owned the land under the mobile home, a Probate proceeding will be necessary to transfer the land to the proper beneficiary. See page 146 for information about transferring real property.

Regardless of whether the mobile home is permanently affixed to the land, title to the mobile home must be transferred in the same manner as any motor vehicle. The new owner must, within 30 days of the transfer, register the home with the Oklahoma Tax Commission (OS 47-1113, 47-1132).

TRANSFERRING AIRCRAFT/WATERCRAFT

The Personal Representative will transfer title to a boat or airplane to the proper beneficiary. If the decedent did not make a specific gift of the boat or plane, the Personal Representative can either sell it or give it to a beneficiary as part of his inheritance. The new owner must obtain his own registration from the nearest Tag Agency within 30 days of the transfer. If no Probate proceeding is necessary, and the decedent's Probate Estate is less than $20,000, the beneficiary of the watercraft can use the Small Estate Affidavit as described later in this chapter, to obtain title to the vehicle.

If you have a question about transferring the boat or aircraft to a new owner you can call the Motor Vehicle Division at (405) 521-3221.

No Probate procedure will be necessary if the decedent owned property in Oklahoma:

⇨ as the owner of a Life Estate - or -

⇨ as a Joint Tenant with right of survivorship - or -

⇨ as Tenant By The Entirety

In each of these cases, the survivor owns the property. If there is a Probate procedure for other property owned by the deceased owner, a title search at the time of transfer will reveal the fact that he died. If Probate is not necessary, the surviving owner needs to get a waiver or a release of the Oklahoma Estate Tax Lien. The release of the Estate Tax lien is not necessary if the surviving spouse is the sole joint tenant or life tenant, or if the decedent has been dead for more than ten years.

Even though nothing need be done to establish the ownership of the surviving owner, consider having an attorney prepare an AFFIDAVIT OF SURVIVING JOINT TENANT with the death certificate attached, saying that the joint owner, or owner of the Life Estate is now deceased (OS 59-912). Once the Affidavit is recorded with the County Clerk in the county where the property is located, the decedent's name is, in effect, removed from the deed.

WHEN PROBATE IS NECESSARY

If the decedent owned Oklahoma property in his name only, or as a Tenant In Common, it will take a Probate procedure to transfer that property to the proper beneficiary. The type of Probate procedure depends on the size of the Estate.

Special Situation

NONPROBATE TRANSFERS OF OUT OF STATE PROPERTY

Each state regulates the transfer of real property within that state. Many states, like Oklahoma, do not require that any document be recorded to transfer real property to a joint tenant who has a right of survivorship, or to a remainder beneficiary of a Life Estate interest. All the Grantee need do is keep a certified copy of the death certificate available to produce at closing when the property is transferred.

Some states allow the death certificate to be recorded in the county where the property is located, so that anyone examining title to the property will know who now owns the property. In other states, an Affidavit of Survivorship is recorded along with the death certificate. If the decedent owned out of state real property jointly with Rights of Survivorship, or if he held a Life Estate interest, you may want to call the recording department in the county where the property is located to find out what documents (if any) need to be recorded to let people know that the surviving joint tenant (or remainder beneficiary) now owns the property. In Oklahoma, the County Clerk is in charge of recording deeds. In other states, it might be the Clerk of the Circuit Court, or the County Registrar or the County Recorder.

Of course, if the decedent owned real property in his own name or as a Tenant In Common, you need to contact an attorney in that state to have the property Probated and transferred to the proper beneficiary.

Any refund due to the decedent under a joint federal income tax return filed by his surviving spouse will be sent to the surviving spouse. If the decedent's Personal Representative filed the final return, then the refund check will be sent to him to be deposited to the Estate account.

If the decedent was single and Probate proceeding is not necessary, whoever is entitled to the decedent's Estate is entitled to the refund check. If you are the beneficiary of the decedent's Estate, you can obtain the refund by filing IRS form 1310 along with the decedent's final income tax return (the 1040). You can obtain form 1310 from the decedent's accountant, or if he did not have an accountant and you wish to file yourself, you can call the IRS at (800) 829-3676 to obtain the form.

You can download instructions, publications and forms from the Internal Revenue Service by going to the FORMS AND PUBLICATIONS section of their Web site.

INTERNAL REVENUE SERVICE
http://www.irs.gov/

The Personal Representative does not need to file form 1310 because once he files the decedent's final income tax return, any refund will be forwarded to him. Similarly, it is not necessary for the surviving spouse who filed a joint return to file form 1310.

THE OKLAHOMA INCOME TAX REFUND

The decedent's final Oklahoma income tax return needs to be filed at the same time the federal income tax return is filed (OS 68-2368). If the decedent was married, his spouse must file a joint or separate return in accordance with the federal income tax return (OS 68-2361). If Probate is necessary, the Personal Representative can file the final tax return. If you have any question about filing the decedent's final return, you can call the Oklahoma Taxpayer Assistance Division at (800) 522-8165.

DEPOSITING THE TAX REFUND

If a joint return is filed, any refund will be sent to his surviving spouse. If the Personal Representative filed the final return, the refund check will be sent to him to be deposited into the Estate account. If no Probate proceeding is necessary and the refund check (or any other check) is in the name of the decedent, you can deposit it into the decedent's bank account. You can get the money in the decedent's account by using whatever Probate procedure is appropriate.

If the amount in the account is under $10,000, you can use the Small Estate Affidavit, as explained on the next page.

THE SMALL ESTATE PROCEDURE

There is no need to go through a full Probate proceeding if the decedent's Probate Estate, not counting mortgages or liens, is not greater than $20,000. For example, suppose all that was owned by the decedent was a bank account with a balance less than $20,000. Oklahoma statute allows the money in the account to be transferred to the proper beneficiary by using a ***Affidavit of Heirship***.

An Affidavit is a written statement, sworn to and signed in the presence of a Notary Public. The Affidavit must say that all of the following are true:

☑ Ten days have passed since the date of death; and

☑ No Probate procedure is pending; and

☑ All taxes and debts of the Probate Estate are paid or provision for their payment is made; and

☑ The value of the decedent's Estate is not greater than $20,000, and

☑ Those who are entitled to inherit the property are identified in the Affidavit.

See the next page for a sample Affidavit.

The beneficiary can give the Affidavit to whoever has possession of your property (bank, securities broker, Department of Motor Vehicles, etc.) and they will turn over the property to him (OS 58-393).

PUBLIC EMPLOYEES RETIREMENT SYSTEM

In Oklahoma, retired public employees are entitled to a death benefit of $5,000. The beneficiary of the decedent's Estate may be able to use an Affidavit of Heirship to collect that benefit (OS 11-49-113.2, 74-916.1).

AFFIDAVIT OF HEIRSHIP
PURSUANT TO OKLAHOMA STATUTE 58-393

1. The undersigned affiant(s), being sworn, state(s) that at the death of the decedent, he/she owned the following described property: PROPERTY VALUE

____

2. The value of the decedent's estate does not exceed $20,000.

3. At least ten days have passed since the death of the decedent and no Probate is pending.

4. All taxes and debts of the Probate Estate are paid or provision for their payment is made.

5. The successor(s) named herein is/are entitled to the payment of any sums of money due and owing to the decedent, and to the delivery of all tangible personal property belonging to the decedent and in the possession of another, and to the delivery of all instruments evidencing a debt, obligation, stock or chose in action belonging to the decedent, in the following respective proportions:

Name of Successor	Address	Relationship To Decedent	Percentage of interest

____

Affiant

Sworn to and subscribed before me on this day ___________

____

Notary Public

If the decedent owned real property or personal property worth more than $20,000, there will need to be a Probate procedure. There is a shortened Probate procedure for Estates worth $150,000 or less or for decedent's who have been dead for five years or more. The Personal Representative can pay all the bills and distribute whatever is left, and ask the Court to simply close the Estate. This is called a ***Summary Administration*** because it can be done quickly, and with little formality.

But there are still basic formalities to be observed such as notifying all creditors that they need to come forward with their claims (demands for payment), and there will need to be a final accounting of monies spent. The Personal Representative will need to employ an attorney to guide him through the process. If no beneficiary or creditor objects, the Court will grant the request for Summary Administration (OS 58-241, 58-245, 58-246).

The Summary Administration procedure can be over within a few months and at a relatively small cost to the beneficiaries, provided there are no problems. However, if:

- ☒ someone challenges the Will
- ☒ there is a dispute about who has the right to inherit the Estate
- ☒ there is an argument about what each beneficiary should receive
- ☒ there is a disagreement about whether a bill should be paid
- ☒ there is not enough money in the Estate to pay all the bills

the Court may order that a full Probate procedure be conducted (OS 58-247).

SUMMARY PROCEDURE FOR SURVIVING SPOUSE

A similar Summary Administration is available to the surviving spouse who is left all of the decedent's Probate Estate and who is named as the Personal Representative of his Will. The procedure is much the same as explained on the prior page, however, there is no limit as to the amount of property that is to be transferred to the spouse (OS 58-1101, 58-1104, 58-1105).

THE FULL PROBATE PROCEDURE

The full Probate procedure is involved and time consuming; not to mention, expensive. Administration of the Estate can take anywhere from several months to more than a year, depending on the size and complexity of the Estate. A Personal Representative must be appointed and Letters issued.

APPOINTING THE PERSONAL REPRESENTATIVE

Oklahoma statute gives an order of priority in the appointment of a Personal Representative. Whoever the decedent named as Personal Representative or Executor of his Will has top priority. Without a valid Will, the Court will use the following order of priority to decide who will serve as Personal Representative.

1st surviving spouse 2nd children 3rd parents
4th brothers or sisters. Those of the whole blood have priority over those of half blood (OS 58-123)
5th grandchildren
6th next of kin who are beneficiaries of the Estate
7th creditors
8th any competent person appointed by the Court

If two or more with the same priority want the job and cannot come to an agreement, then the Court will decide who should serve (OS 58-101, 58-104, 58-122).

YOUR RIGHTS AS A BENEFICIARY

The Personal Representative is in charge of settling the Estate. Too often, beneficiaries of the Estate have no idea of what is going on. They wait to receive their inheritance, not knowing that they have rights under Oklahoma law; and more importantly, not knowing how to assert their rights.

✧ RIGHT TO BE KEPT INFORMED

Anyone who has an interest in the Estate has the right to be kept informed. Before someone is appointed as Personal Representative, you should receive notice that a hearing relating to the appointment of that person will be held no sooner than ten days from the day the notice was mailed (OS 58-128).

✧ RIGHT TO YOUR OWN ATTORNEY

The attorney who handles the Estate is employed by, and represents, the Personal Representative. If the Estate is sizeable, then you might consider employing your own attorney to check that things are done properly and in a timely manner. Even if the Estate is small, consider consulting with an attorney any time you are concerned about the way the Probate is being conducted.

✧ RIGHT TO OBJECT TO PERSONAL REPRESENTATIVE

Regardless of who has priority to serve, it is the Court who has final say as to who will serve as Personal Representative. The judge can appoint the person with priority, or if the beneficiaries of the Estate object, he can appoint someone who is acceptable to those who have a majority interest in the Estate.

Whoever wishes to serve as Personal Representative must be at least 18 years of age. The Court will not appoint him if he has been convicted of an "infamous crime" or if the Court finds him to be incompetent to serve because of drunkenness or lack in understanding or integrity (OS 58-102). The statute does not define "infamous crime" but generally, the Court may decide not to appoint someone who has been convicted of a felony.

✧ RIGHT TO APPEAR BEFORE THE COURT

If you have an objection to the appointment of someone who is asking to be Personal Representative, you have the right to go before the Court and explain your objection (OS 58-129). However, before doing so, you should consult with an experienced Probate attorney. He can explain the best way for you to present your concerns to the Court on this or any other matter. He can tell you what arguments have a good chance of swaying the judge. And he can tell you which arguments have so little probability of success that they are not worth pursuing.

✧ RIGHT TO OBJECT TO THE WILL

You have the right to receive a copy of the Will that is offered for Probate. In Chapter 5 we discussed reasons to challenge a Will. If you have any concern for the validity of the Will, you need to quickly raise these issues.

✧ RIGHT TO DEMAND BOND

It doesn't happen often, but every now and again a Personal Representative will run off with Estate funds. A bond is insurance for the Estate. If Estate monies are stolen then the company that issued the bond will reimburse the Estate for the loss. It is up to the Court to decide whether a bond is necessary, and if so, the value of the bond. The Court will not order a bond if the Personal Representative is an authorized bank or trust company or if the Personal Representative is the sole beneficiary (OS 58-171).

Most Wills state that no bond shall be required. The reason is two-fold. The Will maker chooses someone he trusts to administer the Estate, so he does not think a bond is necessary. And there are economic reasons. The cost of the bond is paid for by the Estate, and ultimately the amount inherited is reduced by the amount paid for the bond. Beneficiaries of the Estate can file a request with the Court to waive bond.

The cost of the bond should not be a factor if there is any danger of the Estate property being lost or mismanaged. If you are concerned about the safety of the Estate assets, then it is important that you not sign a waiver, but rather ask the Court to order the Personal Representative to be bonded.

✧ RIGHT TO KNOW PERSONAL REPRESENTATIVE'S FEES

The Personal Representative is entitled to compensation for his efforts. Oklahoma statute has a schedule of reasonable fees for the Personal Representative based on the value of the Probate Estate:

5% on the first $1,000
4% on the next $5,000
2 1/2% for all amounts over $6,000

Compensation for the Personal Representative is subject to the Court's approval. When awarding fees the Court can take into account extraordinary or unusual services performed by the Personal Representative's. Disputes that must be settled by presenting evidence to the Court fall under this category. For example, if there is a dispute about whether to pay a creditor's claim or if there is an argument about who was entitled to inherit property, the Personal Representative can ask the Court for additional compensation (OS 58-527).

✧ RIGHT TO KNOW THE ATTORNEY'S FEES

It is the Personal Representative's job to use the Probate Estate to pay all valid claims and then to distribute what is left to the proper beneficiary. Debts are paid from the decedent's Estate and not from the Representative's pocket; but if the Personal Representative makes a mistake, he may be responsible to pay for it. For example, if he pays a debt that did not need to be paid — or if he transfers property to the beneficiaries too quickly and there were still taxes due on the Estate, he may be responsible to pay for such error (OK 58-522). The Personal Representative has the right to employ an attorney to guide him through the Probate procedure so that things are done properly and at no personal cost to the Representative. It is proper to have the attorney paid with Estate funds.

You, as a beneficiary of the Estate, have the right to know how much will be charged for legal fees. Ask the Personal Representative to give you a copy of the retainer agreement. If the attorney is employed on an hourly basis, have the attorney give a written estimate of the time he expects to spend on the Probate proceeding.

There is no statutory guideline for what is a "reasonable" fee for the attorney. You could call different law firms and ask what they charge to Probate an Estate with similar assets and that will give you some idea of the going rate. If after doing some "comparison shopping" you believe that the attorney's fee is not reasonable, you can negotiate with them to lower the fee. If you cannot reach an agreement, you can ask the Probate Court to set a hearing to settle the matter.

✧ RIGHT TO COPY OF INVENTORY

Within two months of his appointment, the Personal Representative must prepare an inventory of the assets of the Probate Estate, and where necessary, employ an appraiser to evaluate the property (OS 58-281). The value of the inventory is used to determine the Personal Representative's fees and to determine how much taxes need to be paid. It is important that you receive a copy of the inventory, and that you are satisfied with the value assigned to each item.

✧ RIGHT TO AN APPRAISAL

The Personal Representative can employ an appraiser to assist in determining the value of items included in the Estate inventory — but he is not required to have an appraisal unless ordered by the Court. If you are not satisfied with the value assigned to any Probate asset, you have the right to ask the Personal Representative to have the item appraised. If he refuses, you can ask Court to order an independent appraisal of the item.

✧ RIGHT TO AN ACCOUNTING

Before closing the Estate the Personal Representative must file an accounting of how Estate funds were spent, and how he intends to distribute whatever is left. If the Estate has significant assets you may want your own accountant to look over the accounting. If there are any problems that your accountant can not resolve with the Personal Representative, you can raise these issues with the Court (OS 58-555).

The Personal Representative is not required to file an accounting if all of the beneficiaries waive (give up) their right to an accounting (OS 58-541). You may be asked to sign such a waiver, but are few situations that justify giving up your right to know how Estate monies were spent.

✧ RIGHT TO HAVE THE ESTATE CLOSED WITHOUT DELAY

How long it takes to complete the Probate proceeding depends on the size and complexity of the matter. Your Personal Representative must notify all of your creditors that they have a right to come forward and file a claim for monies owed by the decedent. As explained in Chapter 4, once the Personal Representative is appointed, he will publish a Notice to Creditors in the newspaper for two consecutive weeks. The notice will state that creditors have two months from the first date of publication date of the order to come forward and present their claim (OS 58-331).

The Personal Representative can close out the Estate any time after two months have elapsed from the date of publication of the Notice To Creditors and he has received a certificate saying that all of the taxes have been paid. If an Estate Tax Return must be filed, it might take a year or more before tax clearance is received. The Estate should be closed within a few weeks after the receipt of the state and federal tax release.

If you do not receive an accounting and a proposed plan of distribution within these time periods, you have the right to ask the Court to order the Personal Representative to settle the Estate (OS 58-541).

IT'S YOUR RIGHT - DON'T BE INTIMIDATED

You may feel uncomfortable being assertive with a friend or family member who is Personal Representative. Don't be. It's your money and your right to be informed. Be especially firm if the Personal Representative waves you off with "You've known me for years. Surely you trust me." People who are trustworthy, don't ask to be trusted. They do what is right. The very fact that the Personal Representative is resisting, is a red flag. In such situation, you can explain that it is not a matter of trust, but a matter of what is your legal right.

At the same time, keep things in perspective. Your relationship with the Personal Representative may be more important to you than the money you inherit. The job of settling an Estate can be complex and demanding. If the Personal Representative is getting the job done, let him know you appreciate his efforts.

THE CHECK LIST

We have discussed many things that need to be done when someone dies in the state of Oklahoma. The next page contains a check list that you may find helpful.

You can check those items that you need to do, and then cross them off the list once they are done. We made the list as comprehensive as possible, so many items may not apply in your case. In such case, you can cross them off the list or mark them ***N/A*** (not applicable).

Things To Do

FUNERAL ARRANGEMENTS TO BE MADE

☐ AUTOPSY ☐ ANATOMICAL GIFT

☐ DISPOSITION OF BODY OR ASHES

DEATH CERTIFICATE

☐ HAVE DEATH CERTIFICATE RECORDED

GIVE COPY TO: ______________________________________

____

NOTICE OF DEATH

PEOPLE TO BE NOTIFIED ______________________________

COMPANIES TO NOTIFY

☐ TELEPHONE COMPANY

☐ LOCAL CARRIER ☐ LONG DISTANCE ☐ CELLULAR

☐ NEWSPAPER (OBITUARY PRINTED)

☐ NEWSPAPER CANCELLED ☐ deposit refund

☐ SOCIAL SECURITY

☐ INTERNET SERVER

☐ TELEVISION CABLE COMPANY

☐ POWER & LIGHT ☐ deposit refund

☐ POST OFFICE

☐ OTHER UTILITIES (GAS, WATER) ☐ deposit refund

☐ PENSION PLAN

☐ ANNUITY

☐ HEALTH INSURANCE COMPANY

☐ LIFE INSURANCE COMPANY

☐ HOME INSURANCE COMPANY

☐ MOTOR VEHICLE INSURANCE COMPANY

☐ CONDOMINIUM OR HOMEOWNER ASSOCIATION

☐ CANCEL SERVICE CONTRACT ☐ deposit refund

☐ CREDIT CARD COMPANIES ______________________________

____

____

Things To Do

REMOVE DECEDENT AS BENEFICIARY OF:

- ☐ WILL
- ☐ INSURANCE POLICY
- ☐ PENSION PLAN
- ☐ BANK OR IRA ACCOUNT
- ☐ SECURITY

DEBTS

PAY DECEDENT'S DEBTS (AMOUNT & CREDITOR)

____

COLLECT MONIES OWED TO DECEDENT (AMOUNT & DEBTOR)

____

TAXES

- ☐ FILE FINAL FEDERAL INCOME TAX RETURN
- ☐ FILE FINAL STATE INCOME TAX RETURN
- ☐ RECEIVE INCOME TAX REFUND
- ☐ FILE ESTATE TAX RETURN

PROPERTY TO BE TRANSFERRED

- ☐ PERSONAL EFFECTS
- ☐ MOTOR VEHICLE
- ☐ BANK ACCOUNT
- ☐ CREDIT UNION ACCOUNT
- ☐ IRA ACCOUNT
- ☐ SECURITIES
- ☐ BROKERAGE ACCOUNT
- ☐ INSURANCE PROCEEDS
- ☐ HOMESTEAD
- ☐ TIME SHARE
- ☐ OTHER REAL PROPERTY
- ☐ CONTENTS OF SAFE DEPOSIT BOX

OTHER THINGS TO DO

____

____

____

WHAT TO KEEP — WHAT TO THROW AWAY

Once the Probate proceeding is over, you will be left with many documents and wonder which you need to keep:

COURT DOCUMENTS

You should keep a copy of the inventory to establish the value of property that you inherit. That value becomes your basis for any Capital Gains Tax that you may need to pay in the future. Other than the inventory, there is no reason to keep any Court document, provided you a satisfied with the way things were done; and do not intend to take action against the Personal Representative, or his attorney. The Clerk of the Probate Court keeps the Probate file on record, so if for some reason you later need a copy of a Probate document, you can get it from the Clerk.

PERSONAL RECORDS

The surviving spouse, or if no spouse, his next of kin should keep the decedent's personal papers (birth certificate, marriage certificate, naturalization papers, army records, religious documents, etc.). They may be needed in order to apply for government, or other, benefits. The next of kin may want to keep the decedent's medical records in the event that a family member needs to check out a genetic disorder.

TAX RECORDS

The IRS has up to three years to collect additional taxes, and you have up to seven years to claim a loss from a worthless security, so you should keep the decedent's tax file for seven years from the date of filing the return. You can learn more about which records to keep from the IRS publication 552. You can get the publication by calling the IRS at (800) 829-3676 or you can download it from their Web site: http://www.irs.gov

Everyman's Estate Plan 7

The first six chapters of this book describe how to wind up the affairs of the decedent. As you read those chapters, you learned about the kinds of problems that can occur when settling the decedent's Estate. It is relatively simple for you to set up an Estate Plan so that your family members are not burdened with similar problems. An ***Estate Plan*** is the arranging of your finances for maximum control and protection during your lifetime, and at the same time ensuring that your property will be transferred quickly and at little cost to your heirs.

If you think that only wealthy people need to prepare an Estate Plan, you are mistaken. Each year, heirs of relatively modest Estates, spend thousands of dollars to settle an Estate. A bit of planning could have eliminated most, if not all, of the expense and hassle suffered by those families.

The suggestions in this chapter are designed to assist the average person in preparing a practical and inexpensive Estate Plan, so we named this chapter EVERYMAN'S ESTATE PLAN.

Once you create your own Estate Plan, you can be assured that your family will not be left with more problems than happy memories of you.

AVOIDING PROBATE

After reading the last Chapter, many will come to the conclusion that Probate is a good thing to avoid. Those who have $20,000 or less and no real property may not be concerned with avoiding Probate because as explained in the last Chapter, your beneficiaries can get possession of that property by signing an Affidavit.

But if you own real property, or property in excess of $20,000, in your name only, some sort of Probate procedure will be necessary with all of its inherent delays and expenses. Notice that the operative phrase in the last sentence is *in your name only*. Whether a Probate procedure is necessary depends on how your property is titled (owned). It makes no difference whether you do or do not have a Will. If you own property in excess of $20,000 and that property is titled in your name only, your beneficiaries will need to go through Probate in order to get possession of that property.

As explained in Chapter 5, there are many ways to title real property so that it passes automatically without the need for Probate. For example, if you own real property jointly with rights of survivorship, upon your death, the survivors will own the property without the need to go through Probate. Similarly if you own a Life Estate interest, upon your death, the property passes directly to the owner of the remainder interest.

In this Chapter, we examine ways to title your personal property (bank accounts, securities, etc.) so that it passes to your beneficiaries without the need for Probate.

You can arrange to have all of your bank accounts set up so that should you die, the money goes directly to a beneficiary. For example, suppose all you own is a bank account and you want whatever you have in the account to go to your son and daughter when you die. You might think that a simple solution is to put each child's name on the account as joint tenants with right of survivorship, but first consider the problems associated with a joint account.

⌦ POTENTIAL LIABILITY

If you hold a bank account jointly with your adult child and that child is sued or gets a divorce, the child may need to disclose his ownership of the joint account. In such a case, you may find yourself spending money to prove that the account was established for your convenience only and that all of the money in that account really belongs to you.

⌦ OVERREACHING

If you set up a joint account with your child so that the child has authority to withdraw funds from the account, monies could be withdrawn without your knowledge or consent.

If you open a multiple party account with two of your children, there is the problem of what happens to the funds after your death. Should you die, your share of the account belongs to the surviving joint owners. But as a practical matter each joint owner has free access to the joint account (OS 18-381.39a). After your death the first child to the bank may decide to withdraw all of the money and that will, at the very least, cause hard feelings between them.

Holding a bank account jointly with a family member eliminates the need for Probate, but at the cost of control of the funds. One way to avoid Probate of the account yet retain full control during your lifetime, is to name one or more persons to be the beneficiary of the account. There are two forms of ***Beneficiary Account***.

THE BENEFICIARY ACCOUNT

When you open your account you can direct the bank to hold your account ***In Trust For*** ("ITF") one or more beneficiaries that you name. This type of account is also known as a ***Totten Trust*** (OS 18-381.40a, 6-902). Some people call this a "poor man's trust" because the money goes directly to the beneficiary of your choice without the need to have an attorney prepare a formal (and expensive) Trust Agreement. The only documentation is the agreement that you sign with the bank naming the person of your choice to inherit the money upon your death.

Another type of beneficiary account is the ***Pay On Death*** ("POD") account (OS 71-906). Unless your contract with the bank says differently:

- ⇨ The beneficiary does not have access to the account during your lifetime.
- ⇨ You, as the owner of the account, have complete control over the account. You can add to it or close it or change beneficiaries without asking anyone's permission to do so.
- ⇨ If you name two or more beneficiaries of your account, upon your death, they each will receive an equal share of the account.
- ⇨ If your beneficiary dies before you do, then unless you name an alternate beneficiary, the money in your account will become part of the beneficiary's Probate Estate (OS 18-381.39a).

The Oklahoma law for securities is similar to the statute for banks. You can instruct the holder of the security to Pay On Death ("POD") or to ***Transfer On Death*** ("TOD") to a named beneficiary (OS 71-906). As with the POD account, the Transfer On Death designation has no effect on the ownership of the security until the owner of the security dies (OS 71-907).

The security can be held jointly with another with instructions that once both owners of the security die, the security is to be transferred to a named beneficiary (OS 71-903, 71-908). This is a convenient way of owning a security for the married couple who want a child to inherit the security without going through a Probate procedure.

For example, you can hold a securities account as follows:

TIM REILLY, OLIVIA REILLY, JT TEN
TOD STUART REILLY

which is short-hand for:

> TIM REILLY and OLIVIA REILLY own this security jointly. Once both of them are deceased, transfer this security to STUART REILLY.

If your Estate consists of bank accounts and/or securities only, and you want all of your property to go to one or two beneficiaries without the need for Probate, but with maximum control and protection of your funds during your lifetime, then holding your property in any of these beneficiary forms: *In Trust For*
Pay On Death
Transfer On Death
should accomplish your goal.

GIFT TO A MINOR CHILD

At the beginning of this chapter, we identified two problems with a joint account: potential liability if the joint owner is sued and overreaching by the joint owner. If you wish to make a gift to a minor child, that presents still another problem. The beneficiary account and Transfer On Death securities account avoid the problem of potential liability and overreaching, but if your beneficiary is a minor, there is the problem of the child having access to a large sum of money.

Under Oklahoma law, if the amount in the account is under $10,000, the financial institution may transfer the funds to a trust company or to an adult member of the minor's family. However, they are not required to do so, and may ask for Court authority before transferring the funds. If the funds exceed $10,000, the Court may decide to appoint a Guardian to care for the child's property (OS 30-2-116, 58-1208).

You may think it best that the child inherits more than $10,000 this way a Court will see to it that the monies are held safely till the child is an adult. But that only presents a new set of problems. It takes time, effort and money to set up a Guardianship. If you leave the child a significant amount of money, then the Guardian has the right to be paid to manage those funds. It could happen that the cost of the Guardianship significantly reduces the amount of money inherited by the child. There are ways to avoid the problem of having a Guardian appointed to care for property inherited by a child, and yet ensuring that the monies are protected. One such method is the OKLAHOMA UNIFORM TRANSFERS TO MINORS ACT.

The ***Oklahoma Uniform Transfers to Minors Act*** is designed to protect gifts made to a minor by appointing someone to be the ***Custodian*** of a gift until the child is an adult. For example, you can make a minor child the beneficiary of your life insurance policy and name a trusted relative or friend to be the Custodian of the gift. Should you die while the child is a minor, the insurance company will give the proceeds of the policy to the person you named as Custodian to hold until the child is an adult.

You can make a gift to a minor in your Will. You can appoint your Personal Representative (or anyone else) as Custodian of the gift. For example:

> I give the sum of $20,000 to_______________ (name) as custodian for __________________ (name of minor) under the Oklahoma Uniform Transfers to Minors Act.

LIFETIME GIFTS

You can even use the Oklahoma Uniform Transfers to Minors Act to make a gift during your lifetime of some item such as a shares in a corporation or a limited partnership interest. You can nominate yourself as Custodian of the gift, or you can name another person to serve as Custodian. Once the lifetime gift is made it becomes irrevocable, so this method is not appropriate unless you are sure that you want the child to have the gift once he/she reaches the age of 18 (OS 58-1204, 58-1205, 58-1210).

In general, a lifetime gift must be distributed when the child reaches 18, however you can direct the Custodian to distribute the gift at any age between 18 and 21 (OS 58-1221).

The Custodian needs to invest and manage the property in a responsible, prudent manner. He must keep records of all transactions made with custodial property; and make those records available for inspection by the child's parent, or legal representative, or the child, if the minor is 14 or older. If those records are not to their satisfaction, they can petition (ask) the Probate Court to require the Custodian to give an accounting (OS 58-1213, 58-1220).

The Custodian has the discretion to use the gift to care for the child. The Custodian can pay monies directly to the child, or can use the money for the child's benefit. The Custodian can refuse to use any of the monies for the child and just keep the funds invested until the child reaches 21. If the Custodian wants to keep the funds invested the child's parent, or his legal representative, or the child once he is 14, can ask the judge of the Probate Court to order the Custodian to part with some or all of the money for the benefit of the child. The judge will decide what is in the child's best interest and then rule on the matter (OS 58-1215).

The Custodian is entitled to be paid for his effort each year (OS 58-1216). If the gift is sizeable, the Custodian's fee can be sizeable. Before appointing a person or a financial institution as Custodian, it is best to come to a written agreement about what will be charged to manage the custodial property.

A gift made under the Oklahoma Uniform Transfers to Minors Act is limited to one minor only (OS 58-1211). If you want to give a single gift, such as a gift of real property to two or more children or if you want more flexibility about when the minor is to receive the gift, then a Trust may be the better way to go.

We will discuss Trusts later in this chapter.

THE GIFT OF REAL PROPERTY

As explained in Chapter 5, if you own real property together with another, then who owns the property upon your death depends on how the Grantee is identified on the face of the deed. If you compare the Grantee clause of the deed to the examples given in Chapter 5 you can determine who will inherit the property should you die. If you are not satisfied with the way the property will be inherited, you need to consult with an attorney to change the deed so that it will conform to your wishes.

If you own the property in your name only, when you die, there will need to be a Probate proceeding to determine the proper beneficiary of that parcel of land. If your main objective is to avoid Probate, you can have an attorney change the deed so that upon your death, the property will descend to your beneficiary without the need for Probate. As with bank and securities accounts there are different ways to do so, each with its own advantages and disadvantages.

JOINT OWNERSHIP

If you hold property in your name only, and wish to avoid Probate, you can have your deed changed so that you and a beneficiary are joint owners with rights of survivorship. If you do so, should either of you die, under Oklahoma law, the other owns the property 100%. That avoids Probate, but by making that person joint owner, you are, in effect, making a gift of half of the property during your lifetime. You will not be able to sell that property without the beneficiary's permission. And if the beneficiary gives permission and the property is sold, the beneficiary will have the legal right to half of the proceeds of the sale. As explained on the next page, you may be creating tax problems as well.

You can arrange to sell your home without paying a Capital Gains Tax (see page 40), but if you make someone joint owner of your home who does not live with you, a Capital Gains Tax may need to be paid on the joint owner's share of the proceeds should you decide to sell the property.

CAUTION GIFT OF HOMESTEAD

Some elderly parents worry that they may need nursing care at some time in the future and lose all of their life savings to pay for that care. The parent may decide that the best way to avoid Probate and protect the homestead from loss is to transfer the homestead to their child with the understanding that the parent will continue to live there until he/she dies. But this is just trading risks.

RISK OF LOSS

Property transferred to your child could be lost if the child runs into serious financial difficulties or gets sued. This is especially a risk if your child is a professional doctor, nurse, accountant, financial planner, attorney, etc.). If your child is (or gets) married, this complicates matters even more so. Should the child divorce, the property may need to be included as part of the settlement agreement. This may be to your child's detriment because the child may need to share the value of the property with his/her former spouse. If you do not transfer the property, it cannot become part of the marital equation.

⌧ LOSS OF HOMESTEAD CREDITOR PROTECTION

Up to $5,000 of the value of your homestead is protected from your creditors during your lifetime. That may not seem like much, however, as explained in Chapter 4, should you die, your surviving spouse has the right to continue to live in that house for the rest of his/her life. With the exception of mechanic's liens, property taxes and mortgages on the homestead, none of your creditors can force the sale of the property (OS 31-1, 31-2, 31-6).

If you transfer your homestead to a child, you lose this creditor protection for yourself, and for your spouse. If you transfer your hometo your child and he does not occupy that property as his homestead, then there is no homestead creditor protection whatsoever. The child's creditors can force the sale of the property (that's your home) for relatively small amounts of unpaid debts.

⌧ POSSIBLE GIFT TAX

If the value of the transfer is worth more than $11,000 you need to file a Gift Tax return. For most of us, this is not a problem because no Gift Tax need be paid unless the value of the property (plus the value of all gifts in excess of the Annual Gift Tax Exclusion that you gave over your lifetime) exceeds $1,000,000 (see Chapter 2). But if your Estate is in that tax bracket, you need to be aware that you are "using up" your lifetime Gift Tax Exclusion.

⌧ POSSIBLE CAPITAL GAINS TAX

Although Congress has expressed their intent to phase out the Estate Tax, there is no discussion to do away with the Capital Gains Tax. If you gift the property to the child during your lifetime, when he sells the property he will pay a Capital Gains Tax on the increase in value from the price you paid for your home to the selling price at the time your child sells the property.

If you do not make the gift during your lifetime, the child will inherit the property and receive a step-up in basis, i.e., he will inherit the property at its market value as of your date of death. Under today's tax structure and continuing until 2009, that step-up in basis is unlimited. If your child sells the property when he inherits it, he will not pay a Capital Gains Tax, regardless of how large the step-up in basis. In 2010, there will be a limit on the amount that can be inherited free of the Capital Gains Tax; but that limit is quite high, so for most of us this is not a concern.

⌧ LOSS OF HOMESTEAD TAX CREDITS

As explained on page 41, homeowners who are aged or disabled or who have low incomes are entitled to certain Homestead Tax Exemptions or Tax Credits. If you transfer your home you will lose your the right to a Homestead Tax Exemption or Credit. If you are currently receiving a tax break, it could cost more money in taxes to continue to live in your own home.

Before deciding to transfer your homestead, call the County Assessor and ask whether there will be any tax consequence as a result of the transfer.

⌧ POSSIBLE LOSS OF GOVERNMENT BENEFITS

If you transfer property, then depending upon the value of the transfer, you could be disqualified from receiving Medicaid or Supplemental Security Income ("SSI") benefits for a substantial period of time. When a person applies for Medicaid, he must disclose if, within three years of his application, he transferred property for less than the full value (i.e. he gifted property).

This reporting period extends to five years if the transfer was into or out of a Trust. The Medicaid agency will compute a disqualification period depending on the value of the transfer. This can present a serious problem should you need extended nursing care during that period of time.

Under current state and federal law, there are many ways to protect your homestead and still qualify for government benefits. Before transferring your homestead because of your concern for the cost of future health care, consult with an Elder Law attorney. He will be able to suggest ways to protect your assets, and still ensure that you receive the health care that you may require in your later years.

THE LIFE ESTATE, NOT A COMPLETE SOLUTION

Some of the problems we have discussed regarding an outright gift of the homestead, can be avoided by transferring home but keeping a Life Estate for yourself. However, even though you keep a Life Estate, there still are tax issues and concerns regarding shared control of the property. Before making any transfer of real property, it is important to consult with an Elder Law attorney and/or certified financial planner and/or accountant, to examine all aspects related to the transfer.

☎ LAWYER OUT OF STATE PROPERTY

Each state is in charge of the way property located in that state is transferred. If you own property in another state (or country) then you need to consult with an attorney in that state (or country) to determine how that property will be transferred to your beneficiaries once you die. Many state laws are similar to Oklahoma, namely, property held as JOINT TENANTS WITH RIGHT OF SURVIVOR or a LIFE ESTATE INTEREST are transferred without the need for Probate.

If you own property in another state in your name only, or as a TENANT IN COMMON, or if you own property together with your spouse in a Community Property state, then a Probate procedure may need to be held in that state. If a Probate procedure needs to be done in Oklahoma, then a second Probate procedure may need to be conducted in the state where the property is located. This could have the effect of doubling the cost of Probate.

Still another problem is the matter of taxes. Inheritance taxes may be due in the state where the property is held. It may be necessary to file a tax return in two states. In addition to increased taxes, this can double the cost of the accounting fees.

You may wish to consult with an attorney for suggestions about how to set up your Estate Plan to avoid such problems.

A full Probate procedure may be necessary if you hold property in your name only or as a Tenant In Common. We explored different ways to re-title property to avoid Probate, but these methods may have trade-offs that are unacceptable to you. One way to avoid many of these potential problems is to set up a ***Revocable Living Trust*** (also known as an *Inter Vivos Trust*).

A Revocable Living Trust is designed to care for your property during your lifetime and then to distribute your property once you die without the need for Probate. You may have been encouraged to set up such a Trust by your financial planner, or attorney, or accountant. Even people of modest means are being encouraged to use a Trust as the basis of their Estate Plan. But Trusts have their pros and cons. Before getting into that, let's first discuss what a Trust is and how it works:

SETTING UP A TRUST

To create a Trust, an attorney prepares the Trust document in accordance with the client's needs and desires. The person who creates the Trust is called the *Grantor* or *Trustor* or *Settlor.* We will refer to the Revocable Living Trust as the "Living Trust" or just the "Trust" and the person setting up the Trust as the "Grantor." The Trust document identifies who is to be the Trustee (manager) of property placed in the Trust. Usually the Grantor appoints himself as Trustee so that he is in total control of property that he places into the Trust. The Trust document also names a Successor Trustee who will take over the management of the Trust property should the Trustee resign, or become disabled or die.

Once the Trust document is properly signed, the Grantor transfers property into the Trust. The Grantor does this by changing the name on the account from his individual name to his name as Trustee. For example, if Elaine Richards sets up a Trust naming herself as Trustee, and she wishes to place her bank account into the Trust, all she need do is instruct the bank to change the name on the account from Elaine Richards to:

ELAINE RICHARDS, TRUSTEE OF THE ELAINE RICHARDS REVOCABLE TRUST AGREEMENT DATED JULY 12, 2004.

The bank might ask for a copy of the Trust Agreement, but under Oklahoma law all that is required is that the bank be presented with a *Memorandum* or *Certificate of Trust*. The Certificate of Trust gives basic information relating to the Trust, including the date of execution of the Trust, the Trust tax identification number; the identity of the Settlor, current Trustee, beneficiaries of the Trust, etc. (OS 6-902). Elaine's attorney can prepare a Certificate of Trust at the same time he prepares the Trust. He will include all of the items of information required by state law.

Once Elaine establishes the bank account, all the money in the account becomes Trust property. Elaine (wearing her Trustee hat) has total control of the account, taking money out, and putting money in, as she sees fit. Similarly, if she wants to put real property into the Trust she can have her attorney prepare a new deed with the owner identified as ELAINE RICHARDS, TRUSTEE. See Chapter 5 for an example of real property placed into a Trust.

The Trust document states how the Trust property is to be managed during Elaine's lifetime. Should Elaine become disabled the Trust will provide for her Successor Trustee to take over and manage the Trust funds.

Because the Trust is revocable, if she wishes, Elaine can terminate the Trust at any time and have all the Trust property returned and placed back into her own individual name (OS 60-175.39, 60-175.41). If she does not revoke her Trust during her lifetime, once she dies the Trust becomes irrevocable, and her Successor Trustee must follow the terms of the Trust Agreement as written. If the Trust says to give the Trust property to certain beneficiaries, the Successor Trustee will do so, and without the need for Probate. If the Trust directs the Successor Trustee to continue to hold property in Trust and use the money to take care of a member of Elaine's family, the Successor Trustee will do so.

Setting up a Trust has many good features.

☆☆ AVOID PROBATE

In Oklahoma, Probate can be time consuming and very expensive. Both the Personal Representative and his attorney are entitled to be paid for their services. These fees can be significant. It may be necessary to employ accountants and appraisers, and real estate brokers to sell property as well. If you have property in two states, two Probate procedures may be necessary (one in each state) and that could be costly in time, effort and money. If the Trust is properly drafted and your property placed into the Trust, you should be able to avoid Probate altogether.

☆ CARE FOR FAMILY MEMBER

You can make provision in your Trust to care for a minor child or family member after you die. If your beneficiary is a minor, you can direct your Successor Trustee to distribute the child's inheritance at different times. For example, you can direct your Successor Trustee to give the beneficiary a certain amount of money when he is 18, then 21, then 25, then 30, etc.

If your intended beneficiary has a creditor problem, you can set up a ***Spendthrift Trust*** to protect the Trust funds from the claims of creditors (Property 112.035). You can direct your Successor Trustee to allow Trust funds for your beneficiary's health care, education, and living expenses, and nothing more.

Under Oklahoma law, property you place in the Spendthrift Trust is protected from the creditors of the beneficiary, but not the income. Specifically, Oklahoma law requires that income generated by the Trust be used by the Trustee to pay for the beneficiary's necessities or for back spousal or child support payments. In addition, all income due to the beneficiary that exceeds $25,000, per calendar year, is available to pay monies owed by the beneficiary (OS 60-175.25).

NO CREDITOR PROTECTION FOR GRANTOR

Although you can set up a Spendthrift Trust for the benefit of a family member, you cannot set one up for yourself. Property you place in your Revocable Living Trust is freely accessible to you. It is likewise accessible to your creditors both before and after your death

☆ FEDERAL ESTATE TAX SAVINGS

Many people think that the federal Estate Tax will be phased out so that by 2010, no Estate Taxes will be due regardless of the size of an Estate. But under current law in 2011, the Estate Tax is scheduled to be reinstated and those who own property worth more than $1,000,000 will once again be subject to a sizeable Estate Tax. A couple with an Estate in excess of a million dollars can reduce the risk of an Estate Tax by setting up a Trust, so that each partner can take advantage of his own Estate Tax Exclusion.

For example, if a couple owns two million dollars, they can set up a Trust that separates the money into two Trusts once one partner dies. The Trust can be arranged so that the surviving spouse is free to use the income from both Trusts. Once both partners are deceased, the beneficiaries of their respective Trusts will inherit the funds, hopefully with no Estate Tax due. If the couple does not set up a Trust and continues to hold all of their property jointly, the last to die will own the two million dollars with only one Estate Tax Exclusion available.

✰ PRIVACY

Your Trust is a private document. No one but your Successor Trustee and your beneficiaries need ever read it. If you have a Will, once it is admitted to Probate it becomes part of the County records. Anyone can examine the county records, read your Will and see who you did (or did not) provide for in your Will. Records in the Probate Court (inventories, creditor's claims, etc.) are open to public scrutiny. In some states, Court records are now available on the Internet! (OS 58-718.1, 58-718.2, 58-718.3).

LEASE SAFE DEPOSIT BOX AS TRUSTEE

Another privacy issue is what happens to the contents of your safe deposit box, should you become disabled or die. If you lease a safe deposit box in your name only, should you die, the bank will allow certain people (your spouse, parent, child, grandchild and the Executor of your Will who produces a copy of that Will) to search the contents of your safe deposit box for your Will or Trust. The search must be conducted in the presence of an officer of the bank (OS 6-1308).

By leasing the safe deposit box as Trustee, you can avoid having your family members examine the contents of your safe deposit box. You can instruct the bank that upon your disability or death, your Successor Trustee has full authority to enter the box and remove any and all of the items from that box.

In the event of your death, the bank officer will still need to examine the contents of your safe deposit box. Oklahoma law requires that the bank withhold sufficient funds to pay the Oklahoma Estate Tax, and also that the bank notify the Oklahoma Tax Commission at least ten days prior to allowing your Successor Trustee to take possession of the contents of your safe deposit box (OS 68-812).

☆☆ AVOID APPOINTMENT OF A GUARDIAN

Once you have a Trust you do not need to worry about who will take care of your property should you become disabled or too aged to handle your finances. The person you appoint as Successor Trustee will take over the care of the Trust property if you are unable to do so. If you do not make provision for the care of your property, it may be necessary for a Court to appoint a Guardian of your property. The cost to establish and maintain the guardianship is charged to you. Such legal procedures can be expensive; and once established cannot be terminated unless you die or are restored to health (OS 30-3-116). Guardianship is a good thing to avoid, not only because of the cost of the procedure, but also to avoid a the embarassment of a Court coming to the conclusion that you are not competent to manage your own finances.

With all these perks, you may be ready to call your attorney to make an appointment to set up a Trust, but before doing so there are a few things you need to consider.

THE CONS

⌧ COMPLEXITY

A Trust is a fairly complex document, often more than 20 pages long. It needs to be that long because you are establishing a vehicle for taking care of your property during your lifetime, as well as after your death. Your Trust may be written in "legalese," so it may take you considerable time and effort to understand it.

It is important to have your Trust document prepared by an attorney who has the patience to work with you until you fully understand each paragraph of the document and are satisfied that what it states is what you really want.

⌦ COST

Because of the thoroughness of the document and the fact that it is custom designed for you, a Trust will cost much more to draft than a simple Will. In addition to the initial cost of the Trust, it can be expensive to maintain the Trust should you become disabled or die. Your Successor Trustee has the right to charge for his duties as Trustee, as well as to charge for any specialized services performed. A financial institution can charge to serve as Successor Trustee, and also charge to manage the Trust portfolio. If you decide to have a financial institution serve as Trustee, then it is important to compare fee schedules of different institutions.

If you choose a professional (lawyer, accountant, financial planner, etc.) to serve as Trustee, it is important to have a fee agreement stating what will be charged for his duties as Trustee and what will be charged for professional work done on behalf of the Trust. The agreement should be in writing and signed by you and your Successor Trustee. The fee agreement can be included in the Trust document with a provision that whoever accepts the job of Successor Trustee, agrees to accept the fee as provided in the Trust.

You may decide to appoint your spouse or a family member as Successor Trustee, who may want little, or no, compensation. But regardless of who you choose to be Successor Trustee, you need come to an agreement as to what will be charged to manage the Trust. If you make no provision for fees in your Trust Agreement, then your Successor Trustee has the right to take a reasonable fee from the Trust property. If the beneficiaries of the Trust do not think the fee reasonable, they can ask to the Court to set the fee (OS 60-175.48). But that will probably trigger a legal battle. It is better that you set the fee. Hopefully, that will head off unnecessary legal fees.

⌧ YOU MAY NEED YOUR SPOUSE'S PERMISSION TO TRANSFER PROPERTY INTO YOUR TRUST

Most married couples prepare a Trust as part of their overall Estate Plan. Sometimes a married person has a Trust that was prepared prior to the marriage, or he may decide to create a Trust to care for children from a previous marriage. In such case, it may be prudent to have the spouse agree, in writing, to transfers into the Trust. The reason permission is recommended is the ***Elective Share***. In Oklahoma, the Elective Share is equal to one-half of the value of property acquired by the couple because of their joint efforts. If you leave your spouse less than that amount, then unless your spouse signed a prenuptial agreement giving up the right to that share, he/she can "elect" to take the amount allowed under law and not the amount provided in your Will (OS 84-44).

The astute reader might question what happens to the Elective Share if there is no Probate. Suppose all of the decedent's property is held in Trust, or jointly with someone (not his spouse). If the decedent made no provision for his spouse in his Trust, doesn't that deprive the spouse of his half of property they acquired because of their joint efforts during the marriage?

Oklahoma Courts have been presented with this question and have ruled that because the Trust is under the control of the Grantor until his death, the Trust property is part of the decedent's Estate. As such, the decedent's Trust property is available to make up the Elective Share for the surviving spouse (*Thomas v. Bank of Oklahoma*, N.A., 684 P.2d 553 (Okla. 1984)).

⌧ PROBATE MIGHT STILL BE NECESSARY

The Trust only works for those items that you place in the Trust. If you own property as a Tenant In Common, when you die, a Probate procedure might be necessary to transfer your share of the property to your beneficiary. If you purchase a security in your name only, without a "Transfer On Death" designation to your Trust, then a Probate procedure may be necessary to determine who should inherit the security.

The attorney who prepares the Trust usually creates a safety net for such a situation. He prepares a Will for you to sign at the same time you sign the Trust. The Will makes your Trust the beneficiary of your Probate Estate. If you own anything in your name only, should a Probate procedure be necessary, the Will directs your Personal Representative to make that asset part of your Trust by transferring the asset to your Successor Trustee. Your Successor Trustee will add that asset to your Trust (OK 84-301).

The Will prepared by the attorney is called a ***Pour Over Will*** because it is designed to "pour" any asset titled in your name only, into the Trust. Having the Will ensures that all of your property will go to the beneficiaries named in your Trust. But the downside of holding property in your name only is that a full Probate procedure may be necessary just to get that asset into your Trust. If avoiding Probate is your goal, holding property, in your name only, defeats that goal.

You can ensure that a Probate procedure will not be necessary by transferring your assets into your Trust during your lifetime, but if you neglect to put something into your Trust, the Pour Over Will stands by to transfer that asset into your Trust.

⌧ TAXES MAY STILL BE A PROBLEM:

While you are operating the Trust as Trustee, all of the property held in your Revocable Living Trust is taxed as if you were holding that property in your own name. If the value of your Trust property exceeds the Estate and/or Gift Tax Exclusion value, taxes will be due and owing once you die. For those in that fortunate tax bracket, an experienced financial planner or tax attorney can suggest other, more advanced, Estate Planning strategies to reduce taxes.

⌧ ☆ THE TRUST IS LEGALLY ENFORCEABLE

Any beneficiary of the Trust can petition the District Court to settle a dispute arising out of the administration of the Trust. For example, if the Trustee is not properly administering the Trust, the beneficiaries can petition (ask) the Court to remove the Trustee and appoint another to serve as Successor Trustee (OS 60-175.39).

We gave this section a cross and a star, because the right to have a Trust enforced or administered by a court is a double edged sword. It is great to have the Court protect the rights of your beneficiaries, but the cost of a Court battle could be greater than using Probate to transfer your Estate. Worse yet, your beneficiaries are at a disadvantage because the Trustee can charge the legal expenses to your Trust, while the beneficiaries must pay for their legal battles out of their own pocket. Even if the beneficiaries win the argument, the Trustee's legal fees are paid from the Trust, so there is just that much less for the beneficiaries to inherit.

Although all of the methods discussed in this Chapter can be used to transfer property without the need for Probate, it may be each method has a downside that is objectionable to you. Maybe you don't have enough money to warrant the cost of setting up the Trust at this time. Holding property jointly with another may raise issues of security and independence. Holding property so that it goes directly to a few beneficiaries in a Pay On Death account, may not be as flexible as you wish.

This is especially the case if you wish to give gifts to several charities or to minor children instead of just one or two beneficiaries. For example, if you hold all your property so that it goes to your son without the need for Probate, and you ask him to use some of the money for your grandchild's education, it may be that your grandchild gets none of the money because your son is sued or falls upon hard times. If you keep your property in your name only and leave a Will giving a certain amount of money for your grandchild, the child will know exactly how much money you left and the purpose of that gift.

After taking into account all the pros and cons of avoiding Probate, you may well opt for a Will and a Probate procedure. If you make such a decision, it is important to keep in mind that Estate Planning is not an "all or nothing" choice. You can arrange your Estate so that certain items pass automatically to your intended beneficiary, and other items can be left in your name only, to be distributed as part of a Probate procedure. By arranging your finances in this manner, you can reduce the value of your Probate Estate, and that in turn should reduce the cost of Probate.

Your Oklahoma Will 8

Many people decide that the Will is the best route to go but do not act upon it, thinking it unnecessary to prepare a Will until they are very old and about to die. But according to reports published by the National Center for Health Statistics (a division of the U.S. Department of Health and Human Services) 2 of every 10 people who die in any given year are under the age of 60.

Twenty percent may seem like a small number until it hits close to home as it did with a young couple. They were having difficulty conceiving a child. They went from doctor to doctor until they met someone just beginning his practice. With his knowledge of the latest advances in medicine, he was able to help them.

The birth of their child was a moment of joy and gratitude. They asked a nurse to take a picture of them all together — the proud parents, the newborn child and the doctor who made it all possible. Happiness radiated from the picture, but within 6 months, one of them would be dead.

You might think it was the child. An infant's life is so fragile. SIDS and all manner of childhood diseases can threaten a little one. But no, he grew up a healthy young man.

If you looked at the picture, you might guess the husband. Overweight and stressed out; his ruddy complexion suggested high blood pressure. He looked like a typical heart- attack-prone type A personality.

No, he was fine and went on to enjoy raising his son.

Probably it was the wife. She had such a difficult time with the pregnancy and the delivery was especially hard. Maybe it was all too much for her.

No, she recovered and later had two more children.

It was the doctor who was killed in a collision with a truck.

WHY A WILL IS NECESSARY

Though we all agree, that one never knows, still people put off making a Will figuring that if they die before getting around to it, Oklahoma law will take over and their property will be distributed in the manner that they would have wanted anyway. The problem with that logic is the complexity of Oklahoma's Laws of Descent. If you are survived by a spouse, child, parent or sibling, it isn't too difficult to figure out who will inherit your property. But if none of these survive you, the ultimate beneficiary of your property may not be the person you would have chosen, had you taken the time to do so.

Others think that it is not necessary to have a Will because they have arranged their finances so that all of their property will be inherited without the need for Probate. But money could come into your Estate after your death. This could happen in any number of ways from winning the lottery and dying (of happiness, no doubt) to receiving insurance funds after your death. For example, if you die in a house fire or flood the insurance company may need to pay for damage done to your property. In such case, a Personal Representative may need to be appointed and the monies distributed according to Oklahoma law.

If you die without a Will, the Personal Representative may not be the person you would have chosen. The monies may be distributed differently than you would have wished. And as explained in this Chapter, there are other important reasons to make a Will.

ARRANGE FOR PERSONAL REPRESENTATIVE FEES

In addition to appointing the person of your choice to serve as your Personal Representative, you can come to an understanding about how much compensation he is to receive. If you do not make provision for his fee, then he is entitled to receive the amount as stated under Oklahoma law (OS 58-527). As explained in Chapter 6, that fee is substantial. For example, an Estate worth $200,000 will pay $5,100 in fees to the Personal Representative.

You can put the amount of agreed compensation in your Will; however the job might be more that your Personal Representative expected. He might decide to reject the amount stated in your Will and ask the Court to set his compensation (OS 58-525).

To avoid the problem, you can have your attorney draft an Agreement that you and your Personal Representative sign and attach it to your Will. Having a separate fee Agreement will not stop your Personal Representative from asking for more money, but with such an Agreement, the Court will not agree to the increase unless something unusual occurs (such as a law suit) causing much more work than the ordinary Probate procedure.

You also need to keep in mind that the Personal Representative's fee is just to administer the Estate. It does not include payment for professional work he may do while settling the Estate. If you choose your accountant to serve as Personal Representative, your compensation agreement with the accountant needs to include sufficient compensation for any accounting work he does such as preparing and filing tax returns; preparing an inventory and doing an accounting for the beneficiaries.

A financial planner who serves as Personal Representative may be compensated for his management of the Estate property (buying and selling securities, taking care of rental property, etc.) in addition to his fee to administer the Estate.

But the main problem with appointing a professional as your Personal Representative is the same as appointing a professional to serve as the Successor Trustee of your Trust; namely, that it creates a potential conflict of interest. The professional can use his position as Personal Representative to generate fees that may not have been necessary if someone else settled the Estate. In fact, Oklahoma Courts ruled that an attorney cannot be paid as Personal Representative and as an attorney, saying that it is a conflict of interest for the person appointed as Personal Representative to employ himself or his law firm to do legal work for the Estate (*Matter of Brown's Estate*, 653 P.2d 928 (Okla. 1982)).

When choosing a Personal Representative, consider the relationship of the Personal Representative to the beneficiaries and determine whether it would be better to appoint a non-professional for the job.

CHOOSE A GUARDIAN FOR YOUR CHILD

If one parent dies, it is the right, and duty, of the surviving parent to care for their minor child. But it could happen that both parents become incapacitated or die before the child is grown. If you have a minor child, or an adult incapacitated child, you can appoint someone to serve as the Guardian of the child in the event that both you and the other parent are deceased (OS 30-2-102, 30-3-103). You can even include a Trust in your Will, naming someone to serve as Trustee to care for property that you leave to your child.

MAKE GIFTS OF YOUR PERSONAL PROPERTY

Another benefit to making a Will is that you can make provision for who will get your *personal property* (computers, antiques, securities, boats, etc.). When making a Will consider making provision for your car. If you make a specific gift of your car in your Will, it will be relatively simple for your Personal Representative to transfer the car to your beneficiary. If you do not make a specific gift of your car, then your Personal Representative will decide what to do with it. He may decide to sell it and include the proceeds of the sale in the Estate funds to be distributed as part of the Probate Estate; or he can give the car to one beneficiary of your Estate as part of that beneficiary's share of the Estate.

SMALL GIFTS MATTER

Many who have lost someone close to them report that the distribution of small personal items caused the greatest conflict. If you arrange your finances so that no Probate procedure is necessary, your next of kin will need to decide among themselves how to distribute your *personal effects* (clothing, books, record collection, etc.). Without guidance from you and no Representative with authority to make decisions, there could be disagreement and hard feelings, over items of little monetary value but much sentimental value. If you make a Will, you can include a list of gifts of personal effects in your Will and your Personal Representative will distribute the gifts according to your directions. Of course, you cannot list each and every item you own, but you can instruct your Personal Representative to allow certain family members to take their choice of items not mentioned in your Will. If two or more family members want the same item, have your Personal Representative use an appropriate lottery system (coin toss, high card in a cut of a deck of cards, etc.) to decide who "wins."

MAKE ADJUSTMENT FOR PRIOR GIFTS

You can use your Will to make adjustments for gifts or loans given during your lifetime. For example, if you loaned money to a family member and do not expect to be repaid, you can deduct the loan from that person's inheritance. There is no need to make the adjustment if the borrower gives you a promissory note because should you die, the monies will be owed to your Estate and the Personal Representative can deduct the monies owed from the borrower's inheritance. But if there is no evidence of the debt and you neglect to make a Will, the borrower will receive whatever is allowed under the Laws of Intestate Succession (OS 84-185).

That was the case with Sally and Tom. They were firm believers in treating each of their three children equally. "Share and share alike" was their favorite saying. Once Tom died, Sally continued with the tradition.

Sally did not think of the loan she gave to her son as a gift. After all, he promised to pay it back, with interest. She did not ask her son to sign a promissory note. He was family. If you can't trust your son, who can you trust?

The son was prompt with his monthly payments. But only two payments were made before his mother died suddenly, from a heart attack.

Sally never mentioned the loan to any of her other children. Neither did her son. Each child received one-third of their mother's Estate; and none the wiser.

Except whenever Sally's son dreams of his mother, she is not smiling.

CAUTION YOU CAN'T GIVE WHAT YOU NO LONGER OWN

You need to give considerable thought whenever you make a specific gift to someone. It could be that you no longer own the item at the time of your death. This could happen with property or money. For example, suppose you leave all of your Estate to you son, with a specific gift of $10,000 to each of your three grandchildren. Your son is the residuary beneficiary of the Probate Estate, meaning he gets whatever is left once all of the bills are paid and all of the specific gifts made. If the cost of your last illness leaves your Probate Estate with only $30,000 to distribute, would you want the grandchildren to get their gifts and your son nothing? Of course the simple solution is to make all of them residuary beneficiaries by leaving each a percent of your Estate. For example, instead of making a specific gift to each grandchild you could leave 70% to your son and 10% to each grandchild.

NONPROBATE ASSETS

You can make provision in your Will only for those items held in your name that do not transfer automatically to a named beneficiary upon your death. For example, property held in a Beneficiary Account, Trust property, IRA accounts, life insurance policies will be inherited by your named beneficiary without the need for Probate. You have, in effect, already made a gift of these assets so unless you named your Estate as the beneficiary of these assets, they should not be mentioned in your Will. If you wish to change the beneficiary of a Nonprobate asset, you need to do so during your lifetime and in the manner stated in your contract when you set up the account or insurance policy.

MAKE PROVISION FOR PAYMENT OF DEBTS

Most Wills contain an instruction to the Personal Representative to ". . . pay all the expenses of my last illness, funeral expenses, costs of administration, taxes and just debts. . . " Under Oklahoma law, paying all of your debts does not include paying off a loan on an asset you give to a beneficiary.

For example, if you leave your car to a beneficiary, and you have a loan on the car, you need to specify whether you want the loan to be paid from your Probate Estate so that your beneficiary will inherit the car free and clear, or whether you want to have your beneficiary be responsible to pay off the loan. If make no provision in your Will, under Oklahoma law, your beneficiary will inherit the loan along with the car (OS 84-21).

This same rule applies even if you do not make a specific gift of the item. For example, if there is a mortgage on your home, and you make no mention of who is to inherit the home, then it will be inherited by your residuary beneficiaries; and they will be responsible to pay off the loan.

They can use the Estate funds to do so, but if there is not enough money in the Estate to pay off the loan, whoever takes title to the property will need to pay the debt or make arrangements to refinance the property.

MAKE PROVISION FOR PAYMENT OF TAXES

Taxes are another concern for those Estates large enough to be subject to Estate taxes. State and federal law require that Estate taxes be paid by the beneficiaries of the Estate in proportion to the value received, unless the decedent made some other arrangements to pay for the taxes. If you make no provision for the payment of taxes, whoever inherits your property will pay a percentage of the taxes based on the amount they receive (26 U.S.C. 6324 (a)(2)).

The beneficiary must pay his share regardless of whether he inherits the property through a Nonprobate transfer (joint owner, beneficiary of your Trust, beneficiary of a Pay On Death account, beneficiary of a life insurance policy, etc.) or as the beneficiary of your Probate Estate. (OS 68-802). If a beneficiary refuses to contribute his share of the taxes, under Oklahoma law whoever is required to make payment (usually the surviving spouse or Personal Representative) can ask the Court to order the beneficiary to contribute his share of the taxes.

If this is not as you wish, you can direct your Personal Representative to pay all of your taxes from your Probate Estate. If you do so, beneficiaries of a specific gift, and those who inherit property from a Nonprobate transfer will not contribute to the payment of your taxes. All of your taxes will be paid from your Probate Estate. This means that the amount that your residuary beneficiaries receive will be reduced by the amount of taxes paid.

After reading the past few pages those who do not have a Will may decide that a Will is a good thing to have and decide to sit down and write one out. And you can, because in the state of Oklahoma, if you are at least 18 years old and of sound mind, you can prepare a Will (OS 84-41). You can write one out in your own hand, without the assistance of an attorney. Such a Will is called a ***holographic*** Will. But preparing a Will is like figure skating. It is harder than it looks. A Will needs to be clearly worded. A sentence that can be read in two different ways can lead to a dispute over what you intended; and that could lead to a long and expensive Court battle.

If no one sees you sign your Will, then that presents another problem. Many states have laws prohibiting an unwitnessed holographic Will into Probate. Oklahoma allows a holographic Will to be admitted to Probate provided the Will is entirely written, dated and signed by the Will maker (OS 84-54). But the problem with an unwitnessed holographic Will in this or any other state is its authenticity. If no one sees you sign the Will, how do they know you actually wrote it out? It could be a forgery, or maybe someone was forcing you to sign it.

The problem of authenticity can be solved by having two people witness your signature and then sign the Will saying that they saw you sign the Will and that you acknowledged to them that it is your Will. If the witnesses sign an ***Affidavit*** (a statement signed and sworn to in the presence of a notary public) in the form described in Oklahoma statute (OS 84-55) the Will becomes ***self-proved,*** meaning that the Probate Court can accept your Will into Probate without the need for the testimony of any witness as to its authenticity.

Having two witnesses present when you sign your Will who can testify that you were of sound mind when you signed the Will usually solves the problem, provided the witnesses have nothing to gain from such testimony.

It is important that any witness to you Will is not a beneficiary of your Will or someone may accuse the witness of pressuring you into giving the gift. As explained in Chapter 5, under Oklahoma law a witness is not entitled to the gift unless there are two other competent witnesses to your Will. In the absence of other witnesses, the beneficiary is entitled to only as much as he would have received if you had no Will at all; i.e., according to the Laws of Descent (OS 84-143, 84-144).

Even if there is no undue influence, and the Will is clearly worded, properly signed and witnessed, it can still be challenged if you are married and did not make proper provision for your spouse. Under Oklahoma law your spouse has the right to an Elective Share; which as explained on page 189, is equal to one-half of all of the property acquired during your marriage because of your joint efforts (OS 84-44). If your Will provides less than that amount, your spouse can refuse to take the amount given in the Will and ask the Court for the Elective Share instead.

Although your spouse has the right to elect against your Will, your adult child has no such statutory right. You can give your child as much, or as little as you wish. You have the right to give the child nothing at all.

AVOID A CHALLENGE TO YOUR WILL

If you are concerned that someone may challenge your Will, it is important that you consult with an attorney who is experienced in Estate Planning. The attorney will prepare the Will according to your wishes. If you meet with the attorney in the privacy of his office, and without anyone else present, it will be difficult prove that someone was using undue influence to make you make gifts according to their wishes and not yours.

Once the Will is prepared according to your direction, the attorney can supervise the signing of your Will. He will see to it that your Will is signed and witnessed in the presence of two disinterested witnesses — usually members of his staff. Each witness will sign the Will next to your name as witness; and they will sign a separate paragraph that says, they saw you sign the Will, and you did so of your own free will and at the time you signed it, you were competent to know what you were doing.

Once signed in this manner it will be difficult for anyone to say that you did not know what you were doing when you signed the Will. If your Will is challenged your attorney will be able to present proof to the Court that the Will was prepared exactly as you wished, and that you had full capacity when you signed the Will. You can even have your attorney include a ***no contest*** provision in your Will stating that if your Will is challenged, whoever makes the challenge gets none of your Probate Estate.

Such a provision is called an ***In Terrorem Clause*** because it is designed to cause fear (if not terror) in the heart of your beneficiary. Many states will not enforce such a clause, because they want people to have the right to challenge a Will, and let the Court decide whether that challenge is proper. Under Oklahoma law, a provision that bars a challenge to your Will is enforceable; however, Courts have refused to enforce the clause in cases where there was good cause for the challenge such as forgery, or the existence of a later valid Will (*Matter of Estate of Westfahl*, 674 P.2d 21 (Okla. 1983)).

Including an In Terrorem Clause in your Will, may discourage frivolous law suits. Anyone who makes the challenge understands that if he loses, the Court may find that there was no good reason for making the challenge the first place. Should the Court reach that conclusion, the Court will uphold the penalty provision and the person who made the challenge will be barred from inheriting anything under your Will. But the challenger also knows that if he wins, the Court must conclude that there was good cause to bring the law suit. In that case, the In Terrorem Clause will not prevent him from inheriting property under your Will.

STORING YOUR WILL

Once you sign your Will, you may wonder where to store it. Your attorney may suggest that he place it in his vault for safekeeping. By doing so, he ensures that your heirs will need to contact him as soon as you die. This does not mean that they are required to employ him should a Probate proceeding be necessary. It only means that he will have an opportunity for future employment.

But there are problems with such an arrangement. The Will could be lost or mistaken for another Will. That happened in at least one case. The attorney prepared Wills for two people with the same name and similar family circumstances. When one person died the attorney submitted the wrong Will to Probate.

If you decided to allow your attorney to store the Will, you need assurances that the attorney will be responsible for the document. You should get a receipt and something in writing that says:

- ⇨ The attorney accepts full responsibility for the storage of the Will. Should it be lost or damaged, he will replace the document at no cost to you; and if you are deceased, he will, at no cost to your heirs, present sufficient evidence to the Court to accept a valid copy of the Will into Probate.
- ⇨ There will be no charge to you, or your heirs, for the storage and retrieval of the document.
- ⇨ Should he sell his practice, retire, or die, he or the successor to his practice, will return the original document to you.

You might consider placing your document in a safe deposit box that you lease at a bank. The only problem with the bank safe deposit box is convenient access. If you hold a safe deposit box in your name only, should you die, the bank may restrict access to the safe deposit box. As explained at the end of Chapter 3, the bank may allow a family member (spouse, parent, descendant, Executor of your Will) to inspect the contents of your safe box provided they do so under the supervision of an officer or employee of the company (OS 6-1308).

The bank will allow a Will, Trust, burial plot and insurance policy to be removed from the box. Nothing else can be removed without Court authority. Once a Personal Representative is appointed by the Court, he will have such authority. If you arranged your finances to avoid Probate, it is self defeating to have entry to a safe deposit box trigger a Probate procedure.

For those who are married, the solution to the problem of accessing the safe deposit box without the need to begin a Probate procedure, is to lease the box jointly with your spouse, such that each of you has free access to the box. As explained in Chapter 3, those who have a Trust can solve the problem by giving their Successor Trustee access to the safe deposit box. If you are single and do not have a Trust, you can lease the box jointly with a trusted family member. Of course, if privacy and security are important to you, then that may outweigh any concern for the convenience of your beneficiaries.

Regardless of where you choose to store your Will, let your Personal Representative know that you have a Will and how to retrieve it in the event of your death.

Joint Ownership?
A Pay On Death bank account?
A Transfer On Death Security?
A Will?
A Trust?
A Life Insurance Policy???

Chapters 7 and 8 offer so many options that the reader may be more confused than when he was blissfully unenlightened.

As with most things in life, you may find there are no ultimate solutions, just alternatives. The right choice for you is the one that best accomplishes your goal. This being the case, you first need to determine what you want to accomplish with the money you leave. Think about what will happen to your property if you were to die suddenly, without making any plan different from the one you now have.

Who will be responsible to pay your bills?
Who will inherit your property?
Will Probate be necessary?

If the answers to these questions are not as you wish, you need to work to arrange your property to accomplish your goals.

For those with significant assets — especially those with Estates large enough to pay Estate Taxes, a trip to an experienced Estate Planning attorney may be well worth the consultation fee.

Your Estate Plan Record 9

Once you are satisfied with your Estate Plan, then the final thing to consider is whether your heirs will be able to locate your assets once you are gone.

Most people have their business records in one place, their Will in another place, car titles and deeds in still another place. When someone dies, their beneficiaries may feel as if they are playing a game of "hide and seek" with the decedent. The game might be fun were it not for the fact that an unlocated item may be forever lost. For example, suppose you die in an accident and no one knows you are insured by your credit card company for accidental death in the amount of $25,000. The only one to profit is the insurance company, which is just that much richer because no one told them that you died as a result of an accident.

And how about a key to a safe deposit box located in another state? Will anyone find it? Even if they find the key, how will they find the box?

It is not difficult to arrange things so that your affairs are always in order. It amounts to being aware of what you own (and owe) and keeping a record of your possessions. A side benefit is that by doing so, you will always know where all your business records are. If you ever spent time trying to collect information to file your taxes or trying to find a lost stock or bond certificate, you will appreciate the value of organizing your records.

ORGANIZING YOUR RECORDS

Heirs need all the help they can get. It is difficult enough dealing with the loss, without the frustration of trying to locate important documents. Your heirs will have no problem locating your assets if you keep all of your records in a single place. It can be a desk drawer or a file cabinet or even a shoe box. It is helpful if you keep a separate file or folder for each type of investment. You might consider setting up the following folders:

THE BANK & SECURITIES FOLDER

Store your original certificates for stocks, bonds, mutual funds, certificates of deposit, in a folder labeled BANK & SECURITIES FOLDER. In addition to the original certificate include a copy of the contract you signed with each financial institution. The contract will show where you have funds and who you named as beneficiary or joint owner of the account. If someone owes you money and signed a promissory note or mortgage identifying you as the lender, store these documents in this folder as well.

If you have a safe deposit box, keep a record of its location and the number of the box. Keep a copy of all of the items stored in the box in this folder. If you have an extra key to the box, put it here.

E-bank Accounts If you are doing your banking on-line, it is important to keep a record of your passwords so that your family can access the account in the event of your incapacity or death. The same applies if you have on-line brokerage or installment loan accounts. Keep a paper record of these accounts in this folder.

THE INSURANCE FOLDER

The INSURANCE FOLDER is for each insurance policy that you own, be it life insurance, homeowner insurance, car insurance or a health care insurance policy. If you purchased real property, you probably received a title commitment at closing and the title insurance policy some weeks later when you received your original deed from recording. If you cannot locate the title insurance policy, contact the closing agent and have him send you a copy of your title policy.

THE PENSION AND ANNUITY FOLDER

If you have a Pension or Annuity, then put all of the documents relating to the Pension in this folder. Include the telephone number and/or address of the person to contact in the event of your death.

FOR FEDERAL RETIREES If you are a Federal Retiree, you should have received your **P**ERSONAL **I**DENTIFICATION **N**UMBER (**PIN**) and the person who will inherit your pension (your ***survivor annuitant***) should have his/her own PIN as well. It is relatively simple to obtain this during your lifetime, but it may be difficult and/or stressful for your survivor annuitant to work through the system once you are gone.

Survivor annuitant benefits are not automatic. Your survivor annuitant must apply for them by submitting a claim to the Office of Personnel Management. Your survivor needs to know that it is necessary to apply and also how to apply. You can get printed information about how to apply for benefits from the Office Of Personnel Management (see Page 32). Keep the printed information in this file.

THE DEED FOLDER

Many people save every scrap of paper associated with the closing of real property. If you closed recently on real estate and there was a mortgage involved in the purchase, you probably walked away from closing with enough paper to wallpaper your kitchen. If you wish, you can keep all of those papers in a separate file that identifies the property, for example:

CLOSING PAPERS FOR THE PONCA CITY PROPERTY

Place the original deed (or a copy if the original is in a safe deposit box) in a separate DEED FOLDER. Include cemetery deeds, condominium deeds, cooperative shares to real property, timesharing certificates, deed to out of state property, etc. Also include a copy of related documents such as an Abstract of Title, or a recorded Condominium Approval. If you have a title insurance policy, put the original in the insurance folder, and a copy in this folder. If you have a mortgage on your property, put a copy of the recorded mortgage and promissory note in a separate LIABILITY FOLDER.

LOCATING REAL PROPERTY

If you own a vacant lot, your beneficiaries will find the deed (or a copy) in this folder but that deed will not contain the address of that property because it doesn't have one. The post office does not assign a street address until there is a building on the site. Your beneficiaries can get the location of the property from city or county records. But why make things hard for them? Include a handwritten note in this folder that tells them exactly how to locate the property.

THE LIABILITY FOLDER

The LIABILITY FOLDER should contain all loan documents of debts that you owe. For example, if you purchased real property and have a mortgage on that property, put a copy of the mortgage and promissory note in this folder. If you owe money on a car, put the loan documents in this folder. If you have a credit card, put a copy of the contract you signed with the credit card company in this folder. A lease is a liability, because you have contracted to pay a certain amount for the period of the lease, so include a copy of any lease agreement in this folder.

Many people never take the time to calculate their net worth (what a person owns less what that person owes). By having a record of your assets and outstanding debts, you can calculate your net worth whenever you wish.

THE ESTATE PLANNING DOCUMENT FOLDER

Place your Estate Planning documents (Will, Trust, Antenuptial Agreement, burial, funeral arrangements, etc.) in a separate folder. If you deposited your Will with the District Court, put the receipt for that document in this folder. If you placed you Will in a safe deposit box, place a copy of the document in this folder together with instructions about how to find the original. It is important to keep a copy of your Will or Trust because over the years you may forget what provisions you made. Keeping a copy in your home may save you a trip to the safe deposit box to determine whether you need to update the document.

THE PERSONAL PROPERTY FOLDER

MOTOR VEHICLES

Put all motor vehicle titles in a Personal Property folder. This includes cars, mobile homes, boats, planes, etc. If you owe money on the vehicle, the lender may have possession of the title certificate. If such is the case, put a copy of the title certificate and registration in this folder and a copy of the loan documents in a separate liability folder.

If you own a boat or plane, identify the location of the motor vehicle. For example, if you are leasing space in an airplane hangar or in a marina, keep a copy of the leasing agreement in this file.

JEWELRY

If you own expensive jewelry, keep a picture of the item together with the sales receipt or written appraisal in this folder.

COLLECTOR'S ITEMS

If you own a valuable art or coin collection, or any other item of significant value, include a picture of the item in this file. Also include evidence of ownership of the item, such as a sales receipt or a certificate of authenticity, or a written appraisal of the property.

THE PERSONAL RECORDS FOLDER

The PERSONAL RECORDS FOLDER should include documents that relate to you personally, such as a birth certificate, naturalization papers, marriage certificate, divorce papers, military records, Social Security card, etc. If you have a Power of Attorney or an Advance Directive for Health Care Directive, you can place the document in this folder or in your Estate Planning folder. If you placed the original document in a safe deposit box, keep a copy in this folder together with information about the location of the original.

THE TAX RECORD FOLDER

Your Personal Representative (or next of kin) will need to file your final income tax returns. Keep a copy of your tax returns (both federal and state) for the past three years in your Tax Record Folder.

As explained in Chapter 2, beginning in 2010, there will be a cap on the step-up basis to 4.3 million dollars for property inherited by the spouse and 1.3 million dollars for property inherited by anyone else. It is important to keep a record of the basis of your property, not only for your heirs, but for yourself should you decide to sell the property during your lifetime. If you purchase real property, you need to keep a record of the purchase price as well as monies you paid to improve the property. You will need these records to determine whether there will be a Capital Gains Tax on the transfer. Your accountant can help you set up a bookkeeping system to keep a running record of your basis in everything you own of value.

Many do not have the time, nor inclination, to "play" with all these folders. They do not anticipate an immediate demise. Getting hit by a truck, or dying in a fiery plane crash is not something to think about, much less prepare for. But consider that death is not the only problem. You could take suddenly ill (say with a stroke) and become incapacitated. Even the most time-starved optimist should have a murmur of concern that his loved ones will be left with a mess should something unforeseen happen.

If you do not feel like doing a complete job of organizing your records at this time, consider an abridged version. You can set up a single file with a list of all you own and the location of each item. You need to make that file easily accessible to whomever you wish to manage your affairs in the event of your incapacity or death. You can do this by letting that person know of the existence of the file and how to get it in an emergency; or keep the file in an easily accessible place in your home with the succinct but attention-grabbing title of "***If I Die***."

We have included a form on the next page that you can use as a basis for information to be included in the file.

If I Die

the following information will help settle my Estate:

INFORMATION FOR DEATH CERTIFICATE

MY FULL LEGAL NAME ______________________________

MY SOCIAL SECURITY NO. ______________________________

MY USUAL OCCUPATION ______________________________

BIRTH DATE AND BIRTH PLACE ______________________________

If naturalized, date & place ______________________________

MY FATHER'S NAME ______________________________

MY MOTHER'S MAIDEN NAME ______________________________

PEOPLE TO BE NOTIFIED

____

____

____

FUNERAL AND BURIAL ARRANGEMENTS

LOCATION OF BURIAL SITE

____

LOCATION OF PREPAID FUNERAL CONTRACT

____

FOR VETERAN or SPOUSE BURIAL IN A NATIONAL CEMETERY

BRANCH__________________SERIAL NO.__________________

VETERAN'S RANK ______________________________

VETERAN'S VA CLAIM NUMBER ______________________________

DATE AND PLACE OF ENTRY INTO SERVICE:

____

DATE AND PLACE OF SEPARATION FROM SERVICE:

____

LOCATION OF OFFICIAL MILITARY DISCHARGE
OR DD 214 FORM______________________________

LOCATION OF LEGAL DOCUMENTS

BIRTH CERTIFICATE ____________________

MARRIAGE CERTIFICATE ____________________

DIVORCE DECREE ____________________

PASSPORT ____________________

WILL OR TRUST ____________________

DEEDS ____________________

MORTGAGES ____________________

TITLE TO MOTOR VEHICLES ____________________

HEALTH CARE DIRECTIVES ____________________

Name, telephone of attorney ____________________

LOCATION OF FINANCIAL RECORDS

INSURANCE POLICIES:

Name of Company, Location of Policy, Insurance Agent

____

____

PENSIONS/ANNUITIES:

IF FEDERAL RETIREE: PIN NUMBER: ____________________

NAME OF SURVIVOR ____________________

SURVIVOR PIN NUMBER ____________________

BANK

Name and address of Bank, Account Number,
Location of Safe Deposit Box and Key

____

____

SECURITIES

Name and telephone number of broker

____

TAX RECORDS FOR PAST 3 YEARS

LOCATION ____________________

Name and telephone number of accountant

____

KEEPING UP TO DATE

We discussed people's natural disinclination to make an Estate Plan until they are faced with their own mortality. Many believe that they will make just one Will and then die (maybe that's why they put off making a Will). The reality is, most people who make a Will change it at least once before they die. If you have an Estate Plan, it is important to update it when any of the following events take place:

✍ CHANGE IN MARITAL STATUS

GETTING MARRIED

In the early 20th century, marriage was a simple thing. Two young people fell in love, and married. There was no need for a prenuptial agreement because they came to the marriage with little property and an intent to stay together "till death do us part." Today, young people postpone marriage until they have established careers, so they are coming into the marriage with property that they worked hard to acquire. The intent to remain married remains, but young people are realistic. They know the statistics. Half of the marriages don't work out.

It is a foolhardy couple who enter a marriage in today's society without an ***Antenuptial*** (premarital) Agreement that spells out the rights and responsibilities of the couple in the event one of them dies, or they divorce. An Antenuptial Agreement is legally enforceable in Oklahoma, provided each party makes a full and complete disclosure of his finances and the Agreement provides for the *equitable* (fair) division of property they acquire during their marriage (OS 43-121).

Once the honeymoon is over, it is important to examine your pre-marriage Estate Plan. As explained in Chapter 5, if you do not change the Will you signed before you married, your spouse may be able to challenge that Will, unless your prenuptial agreement gives up statutory rights as they apply to married people.

You should review your Antenuptial Agreement on a regular basis as your finances change or as you have children. With the consent of your spouse, you can amend your Antenuptial Agreement. If it needs a complete revision, you can revoke the agreement, and replace it with a Post-nuptial Agreement. Changes to the original agreement need to be prepared and signed in the same manner as your original agreement. There must be full disclosure by both parties as to the extent of their wealth. It is important that each party be represented by his own attorney.

GETTING DIVORCED

Under Oklahoma law, should your marriage be annulled, or you divorce, and then die before you get around to changing your Will, any gift that you made in your Will for your former spouse is revoked. Your Probate Estate will be distributed as if your spouse died before you die (OS 84-114). A legal separation in the state of Oklahoma does not end the marriage, so these laws do not apply to couples who are separated, legally, or otherwise. If you divorce (or even separate) it is important to review all of your Estate Planning documents (deeds, pension plans, insurance policies, Will or Trust etc.) to determine whether you wish to name a new beneficiary of your property.

✍ A CHANGE IN RELATIONSHIP

If you marry, divorce, have a child, or if a beneficiary of your Estate dies, you need to examine your Estate Plan to determine whether it needs to be revised.

If you decide that your Will needs a complete revision, it is important to have a new Will prepared. If you simply rip up the old Will, that will effectively revoke the Will. But it could happen that someone (perhaps your attorney) has a copy of the Will. If no one knows that you revoked the Will, they may think the Will is lost and offer the copy of the Will for Probate (see Chapter 3). If you draft a new Will, the first paragraph should say, "I revoke all prior Wills ... ."

NOTIFY EMPLOYER OF CHANGE

If you change your marital status (either marry or divorce) you need to tell your employer of the change so that the employer can change your status for purposes of paycheck tax deductions. If you have a health insurance plan or a pension plan, that provides benefits to your spouse, then these need to be changed as well.

FIRE FIGHTERS DEATH BENEFIT

The surviving spouse of an active or retired fire fighter is entitled to a $5,000 survivor's benefit, provided they were married for at least 30 continuous months. The marriage limitation does not apply, if the fire fighter died as a consequence of the performance of his duties (OS 11-49-113.2). If there is no surviving spouse, the benefit goes to whoever the fire fighter named as his beneficiary. The benefit can be transferred without any Probate procedure, so if you are a fire fighter and you marry or divorce, it is important to notify your employer of the change in your marital status.

PUBLIC EMPLOYEE'S DEATH BENEFIT

The Oklahoma Public Employees Retirement System pay a similar benefit to the beneficiary of a retired member. It is important to give the name and present address of your beneficiary, so that they can collect the $5,000 without the need to go through a Probate procedure (OS 74-916.1).

✍ RELOCATION TO A NEW STATE OR COUNTRY

There is no need to change your Estate Plan for a move within the state of Oklahoma. If you deposited your Will with the District Court, you need to retrieve your Will and then deposit it in the District Court of the county of your new residence (OS 84-81, 84-82). If you are moving out of state, you need to take the Will with you. Not all states allow a Will to be deposited with the Court prior to the death of the Will maker. You may need to make other arrangements for the storage of your Will in the new state.

If your attorney has your original Will, or any other of your original documents, then unless you intend to continue to employ him as your attorney, you need to retrieve these originals and take them with you to the new state.

You need to determine whether your Will conforms to the laws of the state of your new residence. Most states will honor a Will drafted according to Oklahoma law, however, the rights of a spouse vary considerably state to state. If you are married and have not provided the minimum amount as required by the laws of the new state, then should you die before your spouse, your Will may be challenged on that basis. The same applies to a Trust. Most states allow a surviving spouse to demand funds from the Trust of the decedent spouse, if the deceased spouse did not provide the minimum amount to his spouse as required by the laws of that state.

If you do not have a Will, then it is important to check out the Laws of Descent for that state. In some states they are called the Laws of Intestate Succession. Each state has its own laws of inheritance and those laws are very different from each other. Who has the right to inherit your property in the state of Oklahoma may be different from who can inherit your property in another state.

If you do not have a Will, this is the time to think about who will inherit your property should you die in the state of your new residence. This is especially important for those who are married. The right of a spouse to inherit property varies significantly from state to state. There is a world of difference in the rights of a spouse in a Community Property state (Arizona, California, Idaho, Louisiana, Nevada, New Mexico, Texas, Washington and Wisconsin) and other states. There is even variation in the rights of a spouse from one Community Property state to another!

OTHER ESTATE PLANNING DOCUMENTS

If you have an Advance Directive For Health Care that is prepared according to Oklahoma law (statute 63-3101.4), you need to determine whether that document will be honored in the new state. The form of a Medical Directive varies significantly state to state. Other states may have laws that enable you to appoint someone with powers similar to your Health Care Proxy, but the laws of the state may refer to such person as a *Patient Advocate* or a *Health Care Surrogate* or a *Health Care Agent,* with the right to make your health care decisions in the event that you are too ill to do so yourself. It is best to sign a new health care document using the forms and terms that are recognized in that state, rather than chance any confusion should you become ill and find yourself in an emergency situation. Similarly, if you have appointed someone to handle your finances under a Power of Attorney to determine whether that document will be honored in the new state.

CREDITOR PROTECTION

Creditor protection is another item that is significantly different state to state. If you have much debt, determine what items can be inherited by your family free of your debts in that state.

TAX CONCERNS

You also need to check out the taxes of the new state. Each state has its own tax structure. Some states have an inheritance tax, or a transfer tax on all inherited property. If state taxes are high, you may need an Estate Plan that will minimize the impact of those taxes.

When moving to another state you need to either educate yourself about the laws of the state, or consult with an attorney who can assist you in reviewing your Estate Plan to see if that plan will accomplish your goals in that state.

✍ BENEFICIARY MOVES OR DIES

Most people remember to name an alternate beneficiary should one of their beneficiaries die. But how many of us remember to notify the pension plan or insurance company when a beneficiary moves? Many life insurance proceeds are never paid because the company cannot locate the beneficiary. The Actuarial Office of the Federal Employees' Group Life Insurance Program reported that as of September, 2003, they had over 55.8 million dollars in unpaid benefits, mostly because they could not locate the beneficiary at the last given address.

✍ A SIGNIFICANT CHANGE IN THE LAW

We pay our legislators (state and federal) to make laws and, if necessary, change those in effect. We pay judges to interpret the law and that interpretation may change the way the law operates. The legislature and the judiciary do their job and so laws change frequently. Tax laws are particularly volatile. The 2001 change in the federal Estate Tax law gradually increases the Exclusion amount so that by 2010 no federal Estate Tax will be due regardless of the value of your Estate.

You may be thinking that there is no need for an Estate Tax plan because you don't intend to die prior to 2010. But any certainty relating to death and taxes is false security (especially taxes, in this case). As explained in Chapter 2, the law as passed in 2001, is effective only until December 31, 2010. If lawmakers do nothing, then on January 1, 2011, the federal Estate Tax goes back into effect; and Estates that exceed one million dollars will once again be subject to Estate Taxes.

And that is not the only uncertainty. Each state has its own Estate Tax structure. It remains to be seen how each state will react to the position taken by the federal government in 2010. If federal Estate Taxes are phased out altogether, some states may follow the lead of the federal government dispense with Estate Taxes. However, with states struggling to balance the budget, more likely they will see this as an opportunity to increase their Estate Taxes, so that Estate Taxes that would have been paid to the federal government will now be paid to the state.

You need to keep up with the news to learn about changes in the law that affect your Estate Plan. It is a good idea to check with your attorney on a regular basis to see if any change in the state or federal law affects your current Estate plan.

You can check out the Eagle Publishing Company Web site for changes we will post to keep this book fresh.
http://www.eaglepublishing.com

Also check out the author's Web site for up dates:
http://www.parman.law.com

We discussed the game of "hide and seek" some decedents play with their heirs. A variation of that game is the "wild goose chase." The person who plays this game is one who never updates his files. His records are filled with all sorts of lapsed insurance policies, promissory notes of debts long since paid; brokerage statements of securities that have been sold, and so on.

When he is gone, his family will become frustrated as they try to hunt down the "missing" asset. If you wish to play this game, then the best joke is to keep the key to a safe deposit box that you are no longer leasing. That will keep folks hunting for a long time!

If you do not have a wicked sense of humor, then do your family a favor and update your records on a regular basis.

Glossary

ABSTRACT OF TITLE An ***Abstract of Title*** is a condensed history of the title to the land. It consists of a summary of all the recorded documents that affect the land, including mortgages.

ADMINISTRATION The ***Administration*** of a Probate Estate is the management and settlement of the decedent's affairs. There are different types of administration. See *Ancillary Administration* and *Summary administration.*

ADVANCE DIRECTIVE FOR HEALTH CARE An ***Advance Directive For Health Care*** is a statement made by someone (the principal) in the presence of witnesses or a written, notarized statement in which the principal gives directions about the care he/she wishes to receive in the event that he becomes too ill to make his own health care decisions. See ***Living Will***.

AFFIANT An ***Affiant*** is someone who signs an affidavit and swears or acknowledges that it is true in the presence of a notary public or other person with authority to administer an oath or take acknowledgments.

AFFIDAVIT An ***Affidavit*** is a written statement of fact made by someone voluntarily, under oath, or acknowledged as being true, in the presence of a notary public or someone else who has authority to administer an oath or take acknowledgments.

AGENT An ***Agent*** is someone who is authorized by another (the principal) to act for or in place of the principal.

ANATOMICAL GIFT An ***Anatomical Gift*** is the donation of all or part of the body of the decedent for the purpose of transplantation or research.

ANCILLARY ADMINISTRATION An ***Ancillary Administration*** is a Probate proceeding that aids or assists the original (primary) Probate proceeding. Ancillary administration is conducted to determine the beneficiary of the decedent's property located within that state, and to determine whether the property is taxable in that state.

ANNUAL GIFT TAX EXCLUSION The ***Annual Gift Tax Exclusion*** is the amount a person can gift to another each year without being required to file a federal Gift Tax Return. The Annual Gift Tax Exclusion is currently $11,000.

ANNUITANT An ***annuitant*** is someone who is entitled to receive payments under an annuity contract.

ANNUITY An ***annuity*** is a contract that gives someone (the annuitant) the right to receive periodic payments (monthly, quarterly) for the life of the annuitant or for a given number of years.

ANTENUPTIAL AGREEMENT An ***Antenuptial Agreement*** (also known as a *Prenuptial* or *Premarital Agreement*) is an agreement made prior to marriage whereby a couple provides for the management of the property during marriage and how their property is to be divided should one die, or they later divorce.

ASSET An ***asset*** is anything owned by someone that has a value, including personal property (jewelry, paintings, securities, cash, motor vehicles, etc.) and real property (condominiums, vacant lots, acreage, residences, etc.).

ASSIGN To ***assign*** is to transfer one's rights to another; for example, a contract may allow the parties to assign their rights under the contract to another person,

ATTORNEY or ATTORNEY AT LAW An ***attorney***, also known as an ***Attorney at law***, or a ***lawyer***, is someone who is licensed by the state to practice law in that state.

ATTORNEY-IN-FACT An ***Attorney-In-Fact*** is someone appointed to act as an Agent for another (the Principal) under a Power of Attorney.

BASIS The ***basis*** is a value that is assigned to an asset for the purpose of determining the gain (or loss) on the sale of the item or in determining the value of the item in the hands of someone who has received it as a gift.

BENEFICIARY A ***beneficiary*** is one who benefits from the act of another or from the transfer of property. In this book we refer to a beneficiary as someone named in a Will, Trust, or deed to receive property, or someone who inherits property under the Laws of Intestate Succession.

BOND A ***bond*** required by the Probate Court is a written document that guarantees the Personal Representative will perform his duties as required by law. The person or company that insures the performance of the Personal Representative is called a ***surety.*** The value of the bond is set by the Court. The cost of purchasing the bond is charged to the decedent's Estate.

BY REPRESENTATION ***By representation*** is a method of distributing property to a group of beneficiaries such that if one dies before the gift is made, the deceased person's share goes to his/her descendants.

CAPITAL GAINS TAX A ***Capital Gains Tax*** is a tax on the increase in the basis of property sold by a taxpayer.

CAVEAT ***Caveat*** is Latin for "Let him beware." It is a warning for the reader to be careful.

CFR *CFR* is the abbreviation for the *Code of Federal Regulations.*

CHOSE IN ACTION A ***chose in action*** is the right to sue, or the right to recover a debt or money

CLAIM A ***claim*** against the decedent's Estate is a demand for payment of a debt of the decedent. To be effective, the claim must be filed with the Probate Court within the time limits set by law.

CODE A ***Code*** is a body of laws arranged systematically for easy reference e.g. the Internal Revenue Code.

COLUMBARIUM A ***Columbarium*** is a vault with niches (spaces) for urns that contain the ashes of cremated bodies.

COMMISSIONER A ***Commissioner*** is someone appointed by the Court or by the government to do a job.

COMMON LAW MARRIAGE A ***Common Law marriage*** is one that is entered into without a state marriage license or any kind of official marriage ceremony. A Common Law marriage is created by an agreement to marry, followed by the two living together, and telling everyone they know that they are husband and wife.

COMMUNITY PROPERTY Certain states (Arizona, California, Idaho, Louisiana, Nevada, New Mexico, Texas, Washington, and Wisconsin) have laws stating that property acquired by husband or wife, or both, during their marriage is ***Community Property*** and is owned equally by both of them.

CONFLICT OF INTEREST A ***conflict of interest*** is a conflict between the official duties of a fiduciary (Guardian, Trustee, attorney, etc.) and his own private interest. For example, it is a conflict of interest for a Successor Trustee to use Trust property for his own personal profit.

CONSERVATOR A ***Conservator*** is someone appointed by the Court care for the property of a person who is determined by the Court to be missing.

CONTINGENT BENEFICIARY A ***Contingent Beneficiary*** is an alternate beneficiary; i.e. someone who inherits if the primary beneficiary dies or loses the right to inherit.

COURT The ***Court*** as used in this book is the Probate Court. When referring to an order made by the court, the term is synonymous with "judge," i.e., an "order of the court" is an order made by the judge of the court.

CREDITOR A ***creditor*** is someone to whom a debt is owed by another person (the *debtor*).

CREMAINS ***Cremains*** is shorthand for ***cremated remains***. It refers to the ashes of a person who was cremated.

CUSTODIAN A ***Custodian*** under the Oklahoma ***Uniform Transfers to Minors Act*** is a person or a financial institution that accepts responsibility for the care and management of property given to a minor child.

DAMAGES ***Damages*** is money that is awarded by a Court as compensation to someone who has been injured by the action of another.

DEBTOR A ***debtor*** is someone who owes payment of money or services to another person (the *creditor*).

DECEDENT The ***Decedent*** is the person who died.

DESCENDANT A ***descendant*** is someone who descends from a common ancestor. There are two kinds of descendants: a *lineal descendant* and a *collateral descendant.* The lineal descendant is one who descends in a straight line such as father to son to grandson. The collateral descendant is one who descends in a parallel line, such as a cousin. In this book, unless otherwise stated, the term *descendant* refers to a *lineal descendant.*

DISTRIBUTION The ***distribution*** of a Trust or Probate Estate is the giving to the beneficiary that part of the Estate to which the beneficiary is entitled.

DURABLE POWER OF ATTORNEY A ***Durable Power of Attorney*** is a document in which the person who signs the document (the ***Principal***) gives another person (his ***Attorney in Fact***) authority to do certain things on behalf of the Principal. The Attorney in Fact is also referred to as the Principal's ***Agent***. The word "***durable***" means that the authority of the Agent continues even if the Principal is incapacitated at the time that the Agent is acting on behalf of the Principal.

ELECTIVE SHARE The ***Elective Share*** is the minimum amount of the decedent's estate that a surviving spouse is entitled to receive under the law. In Oklahoma, the Elective Share is equal to one-half of the value of property acquired by the couple because of their joint efforts. If the decedent's Will does not provide for this minimum value, the surviving spouse can elect to take the amount provided by state law and not the amount provided in the Will.

ENCUMBRANCE An ***encumbrance*** is a claim or a lien or a liability that is attached to real property, such as a mortgage, or lease or a mechanic's lien.

EQUITABLE ***Equitable*** is whatever is right or just. If property is distributed to two or more people equitably, then the division is not necessarily equal, but according to the principles of justice or fairness.

EQUITY The ***equity*** in a home is the market value of the home less monies owed on the property (mortgages, tax liens, etc.)

ESTATE A person's ***Estate*** is all of the property (both real and personal property) owned by that person. The decedent's estate may also be referred to as his ***Taxable Estate*** because all of the decedent's assets must be included when determining whether any Estate taxes are due after the person dies. Compare to Probate Estate.

EXECUTOR An ***Executor*** (feminine *Executrix*) is a legal term found in many Wills. The terms refer to the person appointed by the Will maker to carry out directions given in the Will. In modern Wills, this term has been replaced by *Personal Representative.*

FAMILY ALLOWANCE The ***Family Allowance*** is the amount set aside by the Probate Court to pay for the support and maintenance of the decedent's surviving spouse and dependents during the year following his death.

FIDUCIARY A ***Fiduciary*** is one who takes on the duty of holding property in Trust for another or acting for the benefit of another, such as a Personal Representative, Trustee, Guardian etc.. A fiduciary relationship is also one that is developed out of trust and confidence. For example, an attorney has a fiduciary relationship with his client.

GRANTEE The ***Grantee*** of a deed is the person who receives title to real property from the *Grantor*.

GRANTOR The ***Grantor*** is someone who transfers property. The Grantor of a deed, is the person who transfers real property to a new owner (the Grantee). The Grantor of a Trust is someone who creates the Trust and then transfers property into the Trust. Also see ***Settlor***.

GUARANTOR A ***Guarantor*** is someone who promises to pay a debt or perform a contract for another person in the event that person does not fulfill his obligation.

GUARDIAN A ***Guardian*** is someone who has legal authority to care for the person and/or property of a minor or for someone who has been found by the court to be incapacitated.

HEALTH CARE PROXY A ***Health Care Proxy*** is someone who is appointed by another (the *Principal)* to make medical decisions on behalf of the Principal, in the event that the Principal is to too ill to speak for himself.

HOLOGRAPHIC WILL A ***Holographic Will*** is a Will written, dated and signed by the hand of the Will maker himself. Oklahoma allows a Holographic Will into Probate provided it is written, signed and dated all in the Will makers hand.

HOMESTEAD The ***homestead*** is the dwelling and land owned and occupied as the owner's principal residence.

HEIR An ***heir*** is anyone entitled to inherit the decedent's property under the Laws of Descent in the event that the decedent dies without a Will.

INCAPACITATED The term ***incapacitated*** is used in two ways. A person is ***physically incapacitated*** if he has a physical disability. A person is ***legally incapacitated*** if a court finds that a person is unable to care for his person or property. Once the Court determines that a person is legally incapacitated, the judge will appoint someone to care for the person or property of the incapacitated person.

INDIGENT A person who is ***indigent*** is one who is poor and without funds.

IRA ACCOUNT An ***Individual Retirement Account ("IRA")*** is a retirement savings account in which income taxes on certain deposits and interest to the account are deferred until the monies are withdrawn.

IRREVOCABLE TRUST An ***Irrevocable Trust*** is a Trust that cannot be changed,cancelled or terminated until its purpose is accomplished.

INSOLVENT A person or business is ***insolvent*** if more money is owed than owned, or if the person or business is unable to pay debts as they come due.

INTER VIVOS TRUST An ***Inter Vivos Trust*** (also known as a ***Living Trust***) is a Trust that is created and becomes effective during the lifetime of the Grantor (or Settlor) as opposed to a Trust that he includes as part of his Will to take effect upon his death.

INTESTATE ***Intestate*** means not having a Will or dying without a Will. ***Testate*** is to have a Will or dying with a Will.

ISSUE The decedent's ***issue*** are his descendants, children, grandchildren, great-grandchildren, etc.
See DESCENDANT.

JOINT AND SEVERAL LIABILITY If two or more people agree to be ***jointly and severally liable*** to pay a debt, then each individually agrees to be responsible to pay the debt, and together they all agree to pay for the debt.

JOINT TENANCY In Oklahoma, a ***Joint Tenancy*** means that each tenant owns an equal share of the property. There are no rights of survivorship unless the deed specifically says so.

KEY MAN INSURANCE ***Key man insurance*** is an insurance policy designed to protect a company from economic loss in the event that an important employee of the company becomes disabled or dies.

KEOGH PLAN A ***Keogh Plan*** is a retirement plan available to self-employed taxpayers. Certain tax benefits are available such as tax deductions for annual contributions to the plan. The plan is named for its author, Eugene James Keogh.

LAWS OF INTESTATE SUCCESSION ***The Laws of Intestate Succession*** are the laws of the state relating to who is entitled to inherit the decedent's Probate Estate should he die without a valid Will In Oklahoma, these laws are referred to as the Laws of Descent and Distribution.

LEGAL REPRESENTATIVE A ***Legal Representative*** as related to the Uniform Transfers To Minors Act refers to the minor's Guardian, Conservator, or Personal Representative (OS 58-1202)

LEGALESE ***Legalese*** refers to the use of legal terms and confusing text that is used by some attorneys to draft legal documents.

LESSOR A ***Lessor*** is a person or company who leases property to another (the ***Lessee***). In the case of real property, the Lessor is known as the Landlord and the Lessee as the Tenant.

LETTERS ***Letters*** is a document, issued by the Probate court, giving the Personal Representative authority to take possession of and to administer the Estate of the decedent.

LIEN A ***lien*** is a charge against a person's property as security for a debt. The lien is evidence of the creditor's right to take the property as full or partial payment, in the event that the debtor defaults in paying the monies owed.

LIFE ESTATE A ***Life Estate*** interest in real property is the right to possess and occupy the property for so long as the owner of the Life Estate lives. When the owner of the Life Estate dies, the property will belong to the owner of the ***Remainder Interest***.

LITIGATION ***Litigation*** is the process of carrying on a lawsuit, i.e., to sue for some right or remedy in a court of law. A Litigation Attorney is one who is experienced in conducting the law suit and in particular, going to trial.

LIVING WILL A ***Living Will*** is an Advance Directive For Health Care that gives instructions about whether life support systems should be withheld or withdrawn in the event that the person who signs the Living Will is terminally ill or in a persistent vegetative state and unable to speak for himself.

MEDICAID ***Medicaid*** is a public assistance program sponsored jointly by the federal and state government to provide Medical Assistance for people with low income and limited assets.

NET PROBATE ESTATE The ***Net Probate Estate*** is the value of the decedent's Probate Estate, less all the monies paid to settle the Estate.

NET PROCEEDS The ***net proceeds*** of a sale is the sale price less costs and expenses paid to make the sale.

NET WORTH A person's ***net worth*** is the value of all of the property that he owns less the monies he owes.

NEXT OF KIN ***Next of kin*** has two meanings in law: *next of kin* refers to a person's nearest blood relation or it can refer to those people (not necessarily blood relations) who are entitled to inherit the property of a person who dies without a valid Will.

NON-PROBATE TRANSFER A ***Non-probate Transfer*** is the transfer of property to the decedent's beneficiary without the necessity of a Probate Procedure. This includes property that is transferred to the surviving joint owner, or property transferred to the beneficiary of a Pay-On-Death accounts.

OS ***OS*** is the abbreviation for the *Oklahoma Statutes.*

PERJURY ***Perjury*** is lying under oath. The false statement can be made as a witness in court or by signing an Affidavit. Perjury is a criminal offense.

PERSONAL EFFECTS Personal effects is personal property that is kept for one's personal use such as clothing, jewelry, books, and other items generally found in the home.

PERSONAL PROPERTY ***Personal property*** is all property owned by a person that is not real property (real estate). It includes personal effects, cars, securities, bank accounts, insurance policies, etc.

PERSONAL REPRESENTATIVE A ***Personal Representative*** is someone appointed by the Probate Court to settle the decedent's Estate and to distribute whatever is left to the proper beneficiary.

PETITION A ***Petition*** is a formal written, request to a Court asking the Court to take action or issue an order on a given matter; e.g. a request to appoint a Guardian.

POSTNUPTIAL AGREEMENT A ***Postnuptial Agreement*** is an agreement made by a couple after marriage to decide their respective rights in case of a dissolution or the death of a spouse.

POWER OF ATTORNEY A ***Power of Attorney*** is a document in which the person who signs the document (the ***Principal***) gives another person (his ***Agent***) authority to do certain things on behalf of the Principal.

PRINCIPAL The ***Principal*** of a Power of Attorney is the person who permits or directs another (his ***Attorney-In-Fact*** or ***Agent***) to act for him.

PROBATE ***Probate*** is a Court procedure in which a Court determines the existence of a valid Will. The Decedent's Estate is then settled by the Personal Representative who pays all valid claims and then distributes whatever remains to the proper beneficiary.

PROBATE ***Probate*** is a Court procedure in which a Court determines the existence of a valid Will. The Decedent's Estate is settled by the Personal Representative who pays all valid claims and then distributes whatever remains to the proper beneficiary.

PROBATE ESTATE The ***Probate Estate*** is that part of the decedent's Estate that is subject to Probate. It includes property that the decedent owned in his name only or as a Tenant In Common. It does not include property that was owned jointly with right of survivorship, or in trust for another.

PRO BONO The term ***Pro Bono*** means "for the public good." When an attorney works Pro Bono, he does so voluntarily and without pay.

PUNITIVE DAMAGES ***Punitive damages*** are awarded by a Court to punish someone who deliberately disregarded the rights or safety of another (MN 549.20). It is money awarded in addition to ***compensatory damages*** which are monies awarded to reimburse the wronged person for actual losses.

REAL PROPERTY ***Real property,*** also known as ***real estate,*** is land and anything permanently attached to the land such as buildings and fences.

REGISTERED AGENT A ***Registered Agent*** of a corporation is someone who is authorized to act on behalf of the company and accept service of process in the event the company is sued.

REMAINDER INTEREST The ***Remainder Interest*** in real property is the property that passes to the owner of that Interest, once the owner of the Life Estate dies. See LIFE ESTATE

RESIDUARY BENEFICIARY A ***residuary beneficiary*** of a Will is a beneficiary who is entitled to whatever is left of the Probate Estate once specific gifts made in the Will have been distributed and once the decedent's bills, taxes and costs of Probate have been paid.

RESIDUARY ESTATE A ***Residuary Estate*** is that part of a Probate Estate that is left after all expenses and costs of administration have been paid and specific gifts have been distributed.

RESULTING TRUST A ***Resulting Trust*** is a Trust which is implied by law; i.e., established by a Court, based on the intentions of the parties to a given transaction.

REVOCABLE TRUST A ***Revocable Trust*** is a Trust which can be amended or revoked by the Grantor or Settlor during his lifetime.

REVOCABLE LIVING TRUST A ***Revocable Living Trust*** (also known as an ***Inter Vivos Trust***) is a Revocable Trust that is created and becomes effective during the lifetime of the Grantor or Settlor.

SECURED LOAN A ***Secured loan*** is a loan backed by property. If the borrower does not pay the debt, the lender can take the property. Car loans and mortgages are secured loans.

SELF PROVED WILL A ***Self Proved Will*** is a Will that eliminates some of the formalities of proof in a Probate procedure. The Will is made Self Proved by an Affidavit, signed by the witnesses, in the form as required by the statute.

SETTLOR A ***Settlor*** or ***Trustor*** is someone who creates a Trust.

SIBLING A ***sibling*** is one of two or more people born of the same parents; i.e., a brother or a sister. Unless, otherwise noted, we used the term to include those who have only one parent in common; i.e. a half brother or a half sister.

SOLEMNIZE To ***solemnize*** a marriage is to enter a marriage publicly, before witnesses, rather than privately as in a Common Law marriage.

SPECIFIC GIFT) A ***Specific Gift*** is a gift of a specific item, or part of the Will maker's Estate, that is made to a named beneficiary of the Will.

SPENDTHRIFT A ***spendthrift*** is someone who spends money carelessly or wastefully or extravagantly.

SPENDTHRIFT TRUST A ***Spendthrift Trust*** is a Trust created to provide monies to a beneficiary, and at the same time protect the Trust property from being taken by the creditors of the beneficiary.

STATUTE OF LIMITATION A ***Statute of Limitation*** is a federal or state law that sets maximum time periods for taking legal action. Once the time set out in the statute passes, no legal action can be taken.

STEPPED-UP BASIS A ***stepped-up basis*** is the fair market value placed on property that is purchased or inherited from another. The "step-up" refers to the increase in value from the basis of the former owner (usually what he paid for it), to the basis of the new owner (usually the market value when the transfer is made).

SUCCESSOR TRUSTEE A ***Successor Trustee*** is someone who takes the place of the original Trustee.

SUMMARY ADMINISTRATION A ***Summary Administration*** is a simplified and/or shortened Probate procedure.

SURETY BOND A ***Surety Bond*** is a bond in which a company (the *Surety*) agrees to pay if the *Principal* defaults on his obligation. For example, the Court may order the Personal Representative to be bonded for the value of the Probate Estate. If the Personal Representative does not perform his duties and the Estate loses money, the Court can require the Surety to pay for the lost funds.

SURROGATE A ***Surrogate*** is a substitute; someone who acts in place of another.

TENANCY BY THE ENTIRETY A ***Tenancy by the Entirety*** is the name of a form of ownership of real property held by a husband and wife. It is a joint tenancy with right of survivorship, modified by the common law concept that the husband and wife are one. With a joint tenancy with right of survivor, each joint tenant owns their own share of the property until death, when the surviving owner owns it 100%. With a Tenancy by the Entirety, each owns 100% of the property both before and after death.

TENANCY IN COMMON ***Tenancy In Common*** is a form of ownership such that each tenant owns his/her share without any claim to that share by the other tenants. Unlike a joint tenancy, there is no right of survivorship. Once a tenant in common dies, his/her share belongs to the tenant's estate and not to the remaining owners of the property.

TESTATE ***Testate*** means having made a Will or dying with a Will.

TESTATOR The ***Testator*** is someone who makes and signs a Will; or someone who dies leaving a Will.

TITLE INSURANCE ***Title Insurance*** is a policy issued by a title insurance company after searching title to the property. The insurance covers losses that result from a defect of title, such as unpaid taxes, or a claim of ownership of the property.

TRUST AGREEMENT A ***Trust Agreement*** is document in which someone (the *Grantor, Settlor* or *Trustor*) creates a Trust and appoints a Trustee to manage property placed into the trust. The usual purpose of the Trust is to benefit persons or charities named by the Grantor as beneficiaries of the Trust

TRUSTEE A ***Trustee*** is a person, or institution, who accepts the duty of managing Trust property for the benefit of another.

UNDUE INFLUENCE ***Undue influence*** is pressure, influence or persuasion that overpowers a person's free will or judgment, so that a person acts according to the will or purpose of the dominating party.

UNSECURED CREDITOR An ***unsecured creditor*** is someone who is owed money on a promissory note with nothing to back it up if payment is not made. A ***secured creditor*** holds some special assurance of payment, such as a mortgage on real property or a lien on a car.

WAIVER A ***waiver*** is the intentional and voluntary giving up of a known right.

WRONGFUL DEATH A ***wrongful death*** is a death that was caused by the willful or negligent act of a person or company.

INDEX

G

H

I

N

O

S

W

WEB SITES

PAGE	ORGANIZATION	WEB ADDRESS
79	AARP RESEARCH	http://research.aarp.org
46	Amer. Cncl. Life Insurers	http://www.acli.com
66	Federal Aviation Administration	http://www2.faa.gov
vii	Federal Statutes	http://www4.law.cornell.edu/uscode
70	IRS	http://www.irs.gov
50	Medicare	http://www.medicare.gov
75	Pension Benefit Guar. Corp.	http://wwwpbgc.gov
31	Social Security Admin.	http://www.ssa.gov
52	U.S. Dept. of Labor	http://www.dol.gov/dol/pwba
32	U.S. Office Personal Mgmt	http://www.opm.gov
18	Veteran's Administration	http://www.va.gov
17	Veteran's Admin. Cemetery	http://www.cem.va.gov

OKLAHOMA WEB SITES

151 Oklahoma Statutes are referenced in

Guiding Those Left Behind In Oklahoma

Each state has its own set of laws relating to the settlement of a person's Estate. The laws that are referenced in this book are very different from the laws of other states.

The author is in now in the process of "translating"

Guiding Those Left Behind

for the rest of the states, that is, writing state specific books that explain how to settle the affairs of someone who dies in the given state.

Books for the following states are now in print:

ALABAMA, ARIZONA, ARKANSAS, CALIFORNIA
CONNECTICUT, FLORIDA, GEORGIA, HAWAII, ILLINOIS
INDIANA, IOWA, KENTUCKY, LOUISIANA, MASSACHUSETTS
MARYLAND, MICHIGAN, MINNESOTA, MISSOURI
MISSISSIPPI, NEW JERSEY, NEW YORK
NORTH CAROLINA, OHIO, OKLAHOMA
PENNSYLVANIA, SOUTH CAROLINA, TENNESSEE
TEXAS, VIRGINIA, WASHINGTON, WISCONSIN

Readers of this book can purchase *Guiding Those Left Behind* for $23. This includes shipping and handling.

To order or to check for book availability in other states call Eagle Publishing Company at (800) 824-0823.

- or -

Visit our Web site http://www.eaglepublishing.com

BOOK REVIEWS OF *Guiding Those Left Behind*

ARIZONA

Ben T. Traywick of the Tombstone Epitaph said "This book is an excellent reference book that simplifies all the necessary tasks that must be done when there is a death in the family. There is even an explanation as to how you can arrange your own estate so that your heirs will not be left with a multitude of nagging problems." "The reviewer has been going through probate for two years with no end yet in sight. This book at the beginning two year ago would have helped immensely."

CALIFORNIA

Margot Petit Nichols of the Carmel Pine Cone called it a ". . .TRULY RIVETING READ." " . . . I could scarcely put it down." "This is a book that we should all have, either on our book shelves or thoughtfully placed with our important papers."

FLORIDA

Maryhelen Clague of the Tampa Tribune Times wrote "Amelia Pohl has created a handy, self-help guide that illustrates the necessary steps that must be taken when someone dies, a guide that is easy to read, extremely clear and simple to refer to when the need arises."

NEW YORK

Saul Friedman of NEWSDAY said "And one section that should be read by readers of any age, suggests and describes how to create an 'If I Die' file to point the way to your vital papers and policies, to minimize the problems and costs for your survivors. Alas, not even you boomers will live forever."

OTHER BOOKS BY AMELIA E. POHL

How To Defend Yourself Against Your Lawyer

is a book about the unhappy experiences people have with their lawyers, beginning with that of the author AMELIA E. POHL. She became involved in a law suit and found herself in the role of client, rather than lawyer. She become concerned with lawyers who do not provide clients with the loyalty and respect they deserve. This book is a result of those concerns.

The book is divided into chapters that cover the most common problems that take people to a lawyer: divorce, probate, criminal, personal injury, starting a business, making a Will, buying a house, etc. Each chapter tells of the misadventures of the unwary as they sought the services of a lawyer without a clue as to what they were "buying." This book is funny, sad, interesting, but most of all informative. It tells the reader how to become a savvy consumer, i.e., how to find the right lawyer for the right job. If the reader ever finds the need to employ a lawyer, he will be glad he read this book.

Copyright 2004 272 pages 6" X 9" soft cover
$20 includes Shipping and Handling

Beyond Grief To Acceptance and Peace

AMELIA E. POHL and the noted psychologist BARBARA J. SIMMONDS, Ph.d, have written a book for those families who have suffered a loss.

What to say to the bereaved

- ✧ How to help a child through the loss
- ✧ Strategies to adjust to a new life-style
- ✧ When and where to seek assistance.

80 pages 6" X 9" $10 includes Shipping and Handling

A Will is Not Enough. . .

Many people who have a Will think that they have their affairs in order. They believe that their Will can take care of any problem that may arise. But the primary function of a Will is to distribute property to people named in a Will. A Will cannot:

- ➪ Protect your assets and limit your debt
- ➪ Provide care for a minor or disabled child
- ➪ Avoid Guardianship
- ➪ Appoint someone to make your health care decisions should you be unable to do so
- ➪ Appoint someone to handle your finances should you be unable to do so
- ➪ Arrange to pay for your health care should you need long term nursing care, including qualifying for MEDICAID.

AMELIA E. POHL, Esq. has written a series of state specific books explaining how to do all of these things. This new book series is a continuation of this book. It builds on basic Estate Planning concepts introduced in Chapter 7 of this book and then goes on to introduce other, more sophisticated, Estate Planning methods. Although the topics are sophisticated, the writing style is the same as in this book. It is written in plain English. It is intended for use by the average person.

A Will Is Not Enough is now available for:

ARIZONA, CALIFORNIA, CONNECTICUT, COLORADO
FLORIDA, HAWAII, INDIANA, ILLINOIS, MARYLAND
MICHIGAN, MASSACHUSETTS, NEBRASKA, NEW JERSEY
NEW MEXICO, NEW YORK, OREGON, PENNSYLVANIA
TEXAS, VIRGINIA, WASHINGTON, WISCONSIN.

Readers of this book can purchase *A Will Is Not Enough* for $25. To check for book availability in other states call Eagle Publishing Company at (800) 824-0823.

It is the goal of EAGLE PUBLISHING COMPANY to keep our publications fresh.

As we receive information about changes to the federal or state law we will post an update to this edition at our Web site.

http://www.eaglepublishing.com